HEREWARD SENIOR

D1246419

# The Fenians and Canada

Macmillan of Canada

**Canadian Cataloguing in Publication Data**

Senior, Hereward.
   The Fenians and Canada

Includes bibliographical references and index.
ISBN 0-7705-1628-9 pa.

1. Canada — History — Fenian invasions, 1866-1870.
2. Fenians.    I. Title.

FC480.F4S45                971.04'8                C77-001834-3
F1032.S45

Printed in Canada for
The Macmillan Company of Canada Limited
70 Bond Street, Toronto, Ontario
M5B 1X3

# Contents

# Preface

This work is an effort to examine the Canadian aspects of a movement which ran counter to the forces of isolationism and North American nationalism during the nineteenth century. The continuous stream of Irish immigrants across the Atlantic maintained social and political bonds between Europe and North America which neither the American Declaration of Independence nor the grant of responsible government in Canada could sever. One consequence of this was the emergence of the Fenian Brotherhood, a trans-Atlantic organization active in Britain, Ireland, Canada, and the United States.

Although the purpose of the Fenian organization was to establish an Irish republic, and most North American Fenians were located in the United States, Fenianism became a Canadian problem because of Fenian operations in and against the British American provinces during the crucial years before Confederation. Even though living outside of Ireland, North American Fenians still had a sense of participating in Irish politics. Their attitudes, therefore, towards Canadian and American politics were determined by events in Ireland and, in the case of Canadian Fenian sympathizers, by events in the United States as well. Because Canadian Fenians and many of their sympathizers thought of themselves as part of

an Irish nation overseas, their ideas and actions are difficult
to understand without an extensive examination of the
Fenian movement in Ireland and America.

There have been many studies of the influence of immigration on North American society, but few are concerned with
the links which these movements maintained. In the twentieth
century, these links have been to some extent institutionalized
by Marxist internationalists, Zionists, and various national
and revolutionary organizations. It is far from clear that
trans-oceanic politics are, like the American frontier, a thing
of the past and too soon to say whether the Fenians were
the result of special conditions of the last century or pioneers
of a type of politics destined to survive as long as immigration itself.

Much of the material for this book was collected during a
sabbatical leave made possible by the generosity of the Canada
Council and McGill University, and I wish to express my
gratitude to both. To my wife I am deeply grateful.

HEREWARD SENIOR
*McGill University*

The Fenians and Canada

# CHAPTER ONE

# The Migration of Irish Politics

Fenianism was a development of Irish migration to North America. With large numbers of unassimilated Irishmen in the New World, including an articulate elite of political intellectuals, there would of necessity be efforts to organize support in America for Irish nationalism. Irishmen abroad had been a familiar sight in Europe since the Reformation, and in the eighteenth century Irish brigades had served in the armies of France and Spain, providing an Irish army in exile which in war-time could be the nucleus for an "army of liberation" in Ireland itself.

In America, after the War of Independence, the idea of creating a similar force by organizing Irish units of the American militia was popular among Irish Americans. Yet it was only during periods of tension between the United States and Great Britain, or revolution in Ireland, that there would be talk of using such a force to liberate Ireland or to attack the British American provinces.

While the Irish serving in the armies of France and Spain were Catholic, Irish immigration to North America in the eighteenth century was almost entirely Protestant.[1] Yet these immigrants, like their nineteenth-century successors, were for the most part peasants, driven by economic forces such as British restrictions on Irish weavers, or landlords encouraging

Catholics to bid for leases against established Protestant peasants. Some indication of their relative importance is suggested by the arrival, at the port of Philadelphia in 1729, of 653 British and Germans, about equally divided, and 5,655 Irish. As Irish immigrants extended along the frontier, new townships bearing Ulster place names such as Derry, Tyrone, and Coleraine appeared in the back country of Pennsylvania. In the seaports of Boston and New York the Irish presence began to influence social life, and about 200 Irish settled in Nova Scotia in 1761.[2]

Although there is some evidence of efforts to prevent the sale of land to the Irish, this immigration does not appear to have aroused much nativist sentiment except in circumstances in which the Irish were believed to have been Catholic. It is significant that the Irish Charitable Society of Boston, founded in 1741, did not permit Catholics to hold office or to serve on committees, although they were acceptable as members and eligible for benefits.[3]

The Protestants had left Ireland at a time when interest in the Catholic question was declining following the defeat of the Catholic population in 1690. The Orange societies that had been established during the war period from 1689 to 1713 were withering away, and there was some relaxation of the discriminatory legislation imposed upon Catholics.[4] Yet in America the Irish Protestant immigrants found a rising Protestant zeal. Built on a Puritan foundation, this rising zeal was stimulated by the pressure of the French and Spanish presence in America, and more particularly by the fear of Jesuit missionary work among the Indians and rumours that such work might be extended to the slave population.

These feelings were institutionalized by the anti-Catholic *New England Primer* and children's games such as "Break the Pope's Nose". This popular anti-Catholicism was given intellectual and moral support by sermons and lectures such as the series founded at Harvard by Paul Dudley for "detecting . . . convicting and exposing of the idolatry of the Romish Church; their tyranny, usurpation, damnable heresies, fatal errors, abominable superstitions and other crying wickedness

in her high places,"[5] a series which continued without inter-
ruption until 1857. Such sentiments were also manifested
in laws passed in the various colonies, often presented as
security measures, that forbade Catholics to serve in the
militia and gave magistrates the power to search for and seize
firearms in the possession of Catholics. Legislation of this
kind was resisted by colonial governors and upper houses
through remonstrances and delaying action, an indication
that Catholics had more to hope for from royal prerogative
and enlightened upper classes than from popular movements.[6]

It is evident that any sympathy aroused for Irish nationalism
in America might easily founder on the Catholic question.
Yet Irish nationalism, which emerged in its modern form at
the same time as American resistance to colonial taxation,
was at first entirely Protestant, so much so that "Catholic
Committees" organized at this time in Ireland were not
associated with the parliamentary nationalists or "Patriot
Party", as they were called. Instead Catholics sought to
repudiate their past association with foreign intervention
and conspiratorial politics by stressing their loyalty to the
dynasty and the person of the King. Even peasant secret
societies, which preserved their conspiratorial habits and
went by various names such as "Whiteboys" and, later,
"Defenders" and "Ribbonmen", were non-political in
character.[7]

It is not surprising, then, that extensive bonds of sympathy
developed between the Irish Patriot party and the American
Continental Congress during the 1770s when they were
both opposed to Lord North's administration. Benjamin
Franklin, while visiting Dublin in 1770, was invited to sit in
the Irish House of Commons, a privilege usually reserved
for members of the British parliament.[8]

Most leaders of the American Congress and the Irish Patriot
party regarded laws against Catholics as uncivilized and
unnecessary, but they were unwilling to risk dividing their
parties by making an issue of the Catholic question. This was,
perhaps, more difficult in America than in Ireland because
the Seven Years War had been fought in the new world as a
Protestant crusade. This was evident in the spread to all

the colonies of "Pope's Day", a counterpart of Guy Fawkes'
Day, in which the Pope was burned in effigy. Continental
Congress had no hesitation in harnessing this Protestant
sentiment and found the means of doing so when the Quebec
Act of 1774 secured the position of the Catholic church in
Quebec and at the same time posed a barrier to the westward
expansion of the American colonies. The tone of the attacks
on the Quebec Act suggests that the revolution could easily
have become another Protestant crusade. Lord North's
administration was denounced for establishing in Canada "a
religion that has dispersed impiety, bigotry, persecution,
murder and rebellion through every part of the world."[9]

### IRISH AND AMERICAN INDEPENDENCE

However useful anti-Catholic feeling had been in arousing
opposition to the Quebec Act, its limitations became obvious
when the Continental Army invaded Canada in 1775 and
it became necessary to win over Catholic French Canadians.
Washington ordered the suppression of "Pope's Day" celebrations in the army, and had sufficient prestige to make the
order effective.[10]. Although French Canadians remained
cool to the overtures of the invaders and to the mission of
Father John Carroll, who in 1789 was to become the first
Roman Catholic bishop in the United States, Washington's
action helped clear the way for the alliance with the Catholic
powers of Spain and France in 1778. Yet even this alliance,
which did much to soften American prejudices against
Catholics, did not prevent the various states from retaining
and often strengthening anti-Catholic legislation that had
been passed in colonial times. This legislation survived in
some states well into the nineteenth century in spite of the
fact that the federal constitution recognized no religious
distinctions.[11]

After independence had been gained, the increasingly
Catholic Irish American community, being in need of revolutionary war heroes, found them among Irish Protestants such

as General Richard Montgomery, who had occupied Montreal and then died heroically in an effort to storm Quebec City on New Year's Eve, 1775. Montgomery's ashes were solemnly entombed some forty years after his death in St. Paul's Protestant Church in New York City by Irish Americans who henceforth toasted his name at St. Patrick's Day gatherings.[12]

In their search for revolutionary heroes, the Irish community neglected inconvenient ancestors like the Irish Catholic Volunteers who defended Boston against Washington's army in 1775, and the Royal New York Irish Regiment, which marched on the first recorded St. Patrick's Day parade in New York on March 17, 1777 while the city was under British occupation.[13] Yet these Irish loyalists, like the Catholic Highlanders who settled in Glengarry County, Upper Canada, would give Catholics a stake in the loyalist tradition which would be of significance to the Irish Canadian community.

In Ireland the policy of the "Catholic Committees" was to support British efforts to recruit for the American war. Moreover, Irish Catholics in Britain, as a rule, opposed popular movements.[14] They fought the followers of John Wilkes during the riots of the 1760s and opposed the Chartists in the 1830s and 1840s, even when the Chartists were led by Irishmen like Bronterre O'Brien and Feargus O'Connor.[15]

Yet whatever the sympathies of the majority of Irish Catholics in America at the time of independence, they were in no position to act as a community. In 1785, Catholics in the United States were estimated by Bishop Carroll to number 26,000 in a population of 3,000,000.[16] As little more than half of these Catholics were Irish, the Catholics, although more easily identified as such, were probably a minority even among the first-generation Irish in America.

Moreover, the cause of Irish nationalism was still upheld by the Patriot party in the Protestant parliament in Ireland. At the end of the American War of Independence, the Patriot party had, by demonstrations of the armed and uniformed Volunteers, or "Home Guard", brought about the "Revolution of 1782", which secured limited legislative autonomy for Ireland. The Patriot party leader, Henry Grattan, took up

the cause of Catholic rights, but it was not until the outbreak
of the French Revolution that the Catholics again became a
powerful force in Irish politics.

## THE UNITED IRISHMEN

Under the impression of events in France, there was a revolt
in Ireland of the younger and more radical supporters of
the Patriot party who, led by Wolfe Tone, an energetic
organizer and gifted pamphleteer, founded the Society of
United Irishmen in 1790 and appealed to Catholics to join
in a struggle for Irish independence from Britain. At the
same time, there was a revolt against the clerical and aristo-
cratic leadership of the "Catholic Committee" in Ireland and
members of the hierarchy who supported conservative policies
would soon be abused as "Castle Bishops".

Under the leadership of Joseph Keogh, a "Catholic convention" was held which called for a more active policy and
an alliance with British liberalism. Although the United
Irishmen and the Catholic Committee seemed to have much
in common, and Wolfe Tone for a time acted as the agent of
the Catholic Committee, it was soon obvious that their spirit
was very different. With the outbreak of war with France
in 1793, the Catholic Committee, still cautious, accepted as
satisfactory the Catholic Relief Act of that year, which gave
Catholics the right to vote but not to sit in the Irish parliament. The Catholic Committee then dissolved.[17]

Meanwhile, the United Irishmen decided to gamble on an
uprising in combination with an invading force from France.
This decision led the United Irishmen into the unfamiliar
ground of conspiratorial politics and to an association with
the habitual conspirators in the peasant secret societies. These
societies, which at this time accepted the republicans as their
titular leaders and the republic as their goal, had hitherto
been concerned with the redress of local and particular
grievances. While their support gave the uprising substance,
it also gave it the character of a social revolution and in
some places of a war of religion.

The arrest of United Irish leaders and their failure to
co-ordinate the uprising with an invasion from France limited
the rebellion to a series of local insurrections in the summer
of 1798. In the face of an armed rising of the Catholic
peasantry, the majority of Irish Protestants supported the
Crown and in many cases joined the loyalist Orange Lodges,
while the Catholic peasantry, demoralized by defeat, returned
to traditional non-political secret societies.[18] Moreover, the
union of the British and Irish parliaments in 1801 brought an
end to the Patriot party, which had long been a focus of
Irish nationalism.

Yet it would take time for the impression of these changes
in Irish politics to cross the Atlantic, and the United Irish
Society was able to take root in the United States during the
years immediately preceding the Irish rebellion, when republicanism was a vital force in Ireland. A United Irish Society
was organized with headquarters in Philadelphia which, by
1794, was collecting arms and reprinting pamphlets of the
parent body in Ireland. Members were associated with the
efforts of Genet, an agent of revolutionary France, to make
the United States a base of operations against British
territory.[19] The American United Irishmen also took a lead
in the agitation against the Jay Treaty of 1794 which settled
outstanding differences between the United States and Great
Britain. Their efforts to influence foreign policy provoked
attacks from supporters of the Federalist administration,
which were echoed by William Cobbett, who at this stage of
his career was editing a newspaper in Philadelphia.

By the passage of the Alien and Sedition acts, the Federalist
administration sought in 1798 to suppress all agitation by
supporters of revolutionary France. It is hardly an accident
that the first one prosecuted under the new legislation was
Matthew Lyon, a Vermont Congressman who was also an
active United Irishman. Lyon was a Catholic, but the United
Irishmen in America at this time must have included a substantial number of Protestants. Bishop Carroll cultivated
the goodwill of George Washington, following a policy
similar in some respects to that of the Castle Bishops in
Ireland. Although Carroll would have little sympathy with

agitation against the Alien Act, he could hardly prevent the United Irish from circulating petitions against the Act at church doors.

Yet, in doing this, the United Irishmen managed to involve the Catholic church in the first denominational riot of any dimension in the new republic. This occurred at St. Mary's Church in Philadelphia when a pro-Federalist mob, led by a man named Gallagher, attacked the United Irishmen who were collecting signatures at the church door. Following the pattern of such disputes, there were numerous arrests but no convictions. This relatively minor affair was the subject of a letter from the British Minister to the United States, Sir Thomas Liston, to the Governor of Canada. Liston found that the Federalists were "being shamefully calumniated by some of the popular newspapers; they have ventured to take the law into their own hands, and to punish one of two printers 'by a smart flogging', a circumstance which has given rise to much animosity, to threats, and to the commencement of armed associations."[20]

So strong was Federalist resentment against the United Irish Society that Rufus King, the American Ambassador to the United Kingdom, refused political asylum to the United Irish exiles, Thomas Addis Emmet[21] and Dr. William James MacNeven, commenting that "there were enough republicans in America". These and other United Irish exiles had to await the election of Thomas Jefferson as president before emigrating to the United States. Once there, they formed a nucleus of Irish republican intellectuals who had taken part in Irish history and might conceivably do so again.

Thomas Addis Emmet was the elder brother of Robert Emmet, who had won a place in Irish folklore after his execution for an heroic but futile attempt at a *coup d'état* in 1804, often referred to as "Emmet's rebellon". The elder Emmet, on arriving in America, was admitted immediately to the New York bar, despite the protest of Federalist lawyers. Here he acquired eminence, serving as attorney general for New York State in 1812, but returning to private practice the following year. Dr. MacNeven enjoyed an equally distinguished career

in the medical profession, becoming for a time professor
of chemistry at the College of Physicians and Surgeons.[22]
Among other United Irishmen arriving at this time were the
son of Wolfe Tone, and Herman Blennerhasset, who was
involved in the Burr conspiracy.[23]

These United Irishmen were assimilated easily into
American society but, as long as England was at war, they
nursed hopes of support from the governments of France or
the United States for active conspiracy. Some Americans were
attracted to the idea of a republican crusade to liberate the
remaining European colonies in the American hemisphere.
Yet Spanish, rather than British, territory was the favoured
target for filibustering expeditions. Francesco Miranda, the
Venezuelan liberator, sailed in 1806 with two hundred
men raised in New York for a descent on Venezuela. Burr
conspired to seize Texas in 1805-07 and West Florida was
seized in 1810.

The absence of similar efforts against Canada at this time
suggests that the United Irish exiles rejected the role of
professional exiles and, in spite of their efforts at clandestine
activity in the 1790s, had not become habitual conspirators.
Yet in Canada there was concern about an Irish revolutionary
presence although there was little precise information about
its nature. Lieutenant Governor Peter Hunter of Upper
Canada was warned that an Orange Society in Montreal was
working in conjunction with United Irishmen, an improbable
tale probably stemming from the opposition of the Orange
Lodges to the union of the British and Irish parliaments.
The legislation under which Robert Gourlay was expelled
from Upper Canada in 1819, legislation requiring those
coming into the province to take an oath of allegiance, was
passed originally with the United Irish in mind.[24]

On the eve of the War of 1812, the Irish in the United
States, who still numbered less than 100,000, already had a
small place in American politics, with resident intellectuals,
several benevolent societies, and a small press. The New
York *Shamrock*, or *Hibernian Chronicle*, carrying on its
masthead the Harp and the American Eagle, could announce
confidently that the Irish would do their part in the ensuing

conflict.[25] Meeting on July 4, 1812, the Hibernian Society
and the Tammany Club pledged toasts to the memory of
General Montgomery and to the hope that England, Scotland,
and Ireland would soon be republics.[26]

Ireland would be rescued, the *Shamrock* editor declared,
"on the plains of Canada". Irishmen should avenge past
wrongs and prove their loyalty to their new country by enlist-
ing, and it was pointed out that the "best legions of bravest
Caesars were never clothed as well as the American army
would be."[26] Yet Irishmen who had not become American
citizens and were consequently still British subjects would
have to register and were advised to do so by the *Shamrock*.
When companies of "Irishmen and descendants of Irishmen"
were recruited in Baltimore, the *Shamrock* commented that
"Some say these distinctions ought not to be made. . . . we say
it ought. . . . it will give an instance of devotion to the
cause of America." There were alien Irishmen, "who could
not assume the name of Americans", prepared to "annihilate
the powers of Britain and her savage allies in Canada."[27]

These efforts to assert an Irish American patriotism by
support of what soon became an unpopular war aroused
further resentment among conservative Americans. At the
Hartford Convention, designed to bring the war to an end,
the question of limiting the rights of naturalized Americans
to hold office was discussed with the Irish in mind.[28]

POST-WAR IMMIGRATION AND THE CATHOLIC QUESTION

Although the small Irish American community had been a
political irritant before 1812, it was hardly a social problem.
Nor was it yet a "Catholic problem", as most of the United
Irish exiles had been of Protestant background. Immigration
had been virtually suspended during the war years, but after
1815 accelerating waves of immigrants became an agency of
social change in North America, reaching revolutionary pro-
portions during the years 1828-32 and in the years immediately
after the Irish potato famine of 1845. It is not surprising, then,
that the breaking of the first immigrant wave in the 1830s was

followed by an outburst of nativism in both the British provinces and the American republic, and that the famine-crisis
immigration of the mid-forties was followed by the organization of the nativist "Know-Nothing party" in the United
States. Immigrant labour posed an obvious threat to established
living standards and, because of the excessive drinking, rioting, and conviction for crime associated with immigrants, a
threat to moral standards as well. In politics, immigrants dis-
rupted existing voting patterns by their bloc votes which were
denounced as an instrument of corruption and alien influence.

As the most conspicuous group of immigrants were Catholic
and the majority of these were Irish, immigration posed a cul-
tural problem which alarmed Protestant clergy, who considered
the permanence of a substantial Protestant majority as essential to the preservation of the established framework of American society. The extent of this threat was measured in the
expansion of the Catholic church from a small community with
a single bishop at the turn of the century to ten dioceses, supported by six seminaries, nine colleges, and thirty monasteries,
and houses of worship for religious women by mid-century.
Moreover, the church was taking root in the West.[29] Ohio,
which became a state in 1802, could claim twenty-two Catholic
churches, a newspaper, and a seminary. In many of the Western
states and territories, as in the British provinces, Catholics
formed a conspicuous element among the first settlers and
consequently could not easily be treated as outsiders or aliens.

Catholic Americans were ceasing to be a tolerated minority
and, under the influence of the Papal Jubilee of Leo XII in
1827, they were seeking to win converts and becoming a formidable moral force in American society.[30] This Catholic religious
revival inevitably clashed with the Protestant evangelicals who
considered missionary work among Catholic immigrants a
necessary means of Americanization.

During these years the Catholic church in America was coming increasingly under the influence of first-generation Irish
clergy such as John England, Bishop of Charleston. Bishop
England, who was born in County Cork in 1786 and became
an American citizen in 1826, like most of his generation
favoured Americanization of the church, but found this diffi-

cult to effect without surrendering to secular and Protestant influences.[31] There was the Hoganite controversy which arose when the trustees of the Cathedral of Baltimore challenged the right of the bishop to appoint cathedral clergy. Hogan, the priest favoured by the trustees, was excommunicated and his supporters sought public sympathy, stressing their wish to exclude foreign influence.[32]

The fear of secret organizations with foreign connections, which led to the transitory "anti-Masonic" party in the 1820s, was also directed against the Catholic church, which seemed to be associated with attitudes and traditions likely to undermine republican institutions. Such feelings were undoubtedly strengthened by the appearance of the *Catholic Diary* in New York; the *Catholic Telegraph* in Cincinnati; and *The Jesuit* (which soon changed its name to *The Pilot*) , the *Diary,* and *Freeman's Journal,* all in Boston. This "Irish press" drew on the literary talents of clerical, as well as secular, journalists. Although surviving United Irishmen contributed to these journals, the journals reflected the politics of contemporary Ireland rather than the politics of the generation of 1798.[33]

The peasantry, who supplied the vast majority of the immigrants, preserved the memories of 1798, but they saw the Irish rebellion as part of a historic struggle with Britain and the Protestant Irish, rather a republican movement. The various peasant secret and fraternal societies, which took their signs and passwords across the Atlantic, were non-political in character. They tried to redress local and particular grievances and were ready to fight Orangemen or to use terrorism against personal enemies, but they were little attracted by general ideas and larger political schemes. Many of these societies, including the "Molly Maguires" who terrorized the Pennsylvania coalfields in the 1870s, were affiliated with the highly respectable Ancient Order of Hibernians. So far were such groups from being doctrinaire republicans that the Molly Maguires drank the health of the ultra-Catholic pretender to the Spanish throne — Don Carlos.[34]

The secrecy and violence of these societies were condemned by the church and by Daniel O'Connell, who, emerging as the leading figure in Irish politics in the 1820s, captured the imagi-

nation of the Irish at home and abroad for over a generation.
O'Connell had taken up the Irish nationalism of the old
Patriot party, but had given priority to Catholic emancipation as a matter of political necessity. While he paid the custo-
mary tribute to the heroism of the men of 1798, O'Connell
rejected republicanism as a system of government, and rejected
conspiracy as a political weapon. He also rejected the political
conservatism of the Castle Bishops and took up the policy of
political agitation and an alliance with British radicalism
which Joseph Keogh had contemplated in 1793.

O'Connell's strength lay in his ability to use the resources
of the clergy to support the efforts of liberal journalists and
parliamentarians to secure Catholic rights. His success in winning Catholic emancipation in 1829 marked the first victory
for popular agitation since the French Revolution, giving
O'Connell an international reputation. Yet if O'Connell was
a great agitator, he was also a conventional politician, who
after his victory in 1829 organized an Irish bloc vote in the
British parliament and, during the years 1835-41, which covered the period of the Canadian rebellions, supported the
government of Lord Melbourne in return for specific concessions.[35]

## FRIENDS OF IRELAND

Like the republicanism of 1798, O'Connellism crossed the
Atlantic in the form of societies, styled "The Friends of Ireland", which were designed to secure support for O'Connell's
Catholic Association in Ireland. Unlike the United Irishmen,
such societies could be organized legally in both the British
provinces and the United States. The organization of these
societies even extended to the French-speaking town of Trois
Rivières where a Société des Amis d'Irlande was formed on
January 21, 1829.[36] However much O'Connell's vigorous agitation might alarm some conservatives, Canadian reformers could
offer moral support for O'Connell without suspicion of treason,
and American Democrats could do so without approving conspiracy or creating difficulties for American foreign policy.

Nevertheless, meetings of the Friends of Ireland tended to attract disaffected persons and seemed to provide additional evidence, in the United States at least, of Catholic power and influence.

O'Connell's campaign provoked a Protestant reaction in the United Kingdom. This resulted in a flood of anti-Catholic literature which found eager imitators and readers in the United States. In the Canadian provinces, as will be shown later, the Catholic question was obscured by the more pressing issues of nativism and loyalism, but in the United States the 1830s saw the convergence of anti-Catholic and nativist sentiment that reached a kind of climax in the burning of the Ursuline convent near Boston in 1834. Modelled after a similar institution in Quebec City, the convent offered education to upper- and middle-class young women, and its qualities as an educational institution had attracted a few Protestants. The convent was criticized frequently from Protestant pulpits, particularly that of Lyman Beecher, father of the great abolitionist, Henry Ward Beecher. Such sermons appear to have unwittingly harnessed the resentment of lower-class Protestants who felt the competition of immigrant labour and resented the convent as an institution of upper-class learning.

At the time that the convent was ransacked and burned in the presence of helpless magistrates, there were sixty female children and ten adults in it. Conviction of those accused of the burning proved impossible and subsequent efforts to collect damages were defeated by agitation against giving public money to religious institutions. As the American *Protestant Vindicator* put it, the "Treasury of the descendants of Puritans" should not provide funds for Ursuline nunneries which could serve as a headquarters for the bishop and "his 20,000 violent Irishmen".[37]

Although Protestant clergy and journalists denounced mob violence against Catholics, their propaganda campaign continued. Catholic congregations were soon taking measures to protect their churches, and it became impossible to secure fire insurance except for those churches built of non-combustible material.

In 1836 Reverend H. K. Hoyt sponsored the publication of the lurid confessions of Maria Monk, purporting to be the adventures of a young woman in the Hotel Dieu, Montreal.[38] The circulation of this and similar works, along with the burning of the convent, which took place during the decade of the Canadian rebellions of 1837-38, must have reminded the Irish that they too could be attacked in the name of that "Americanism" which, in 1798 and 1812, they had tried to turn against the British presence in North America.

## THE IRISH IN CANADA

The arrival of O'Connellite journalists in Canada marked the effective beginning of Irish Canadian politics. As these journalists shared the views of Canadian Reformers, they seemed destined to lead the Irish immigrants into an alliance with Canadian liberalism in much the same way as the Irish Americans had been led into an alliance with Jeffersonian democracy. O'Connell was highly respected by Papineau, and the Patriote party included references to O'Connell in the "92 Resolutions" introduced into the Lower Canadian Assembly in 1834.[39] In Upper Canada, William Lyon Mackenzie appealed to Irish immigrants in the name of O'Connell. Yet the program of the Reform party, which Canadian O'Connellites adopted, could not be reconciled with the interests of the Irish immigrants.

Both the Patriote party and Mackenzie's wing of the Reform party were based on the native or, in the case of Upper Canada, the North American-born population. Papineau himself adopted his own form of "Americanism", writing to his colleague, the Scottish-born John Neilson, that the struggle for reform was a conflict between Europeans and Americans.[40] Yet the alliance between the Reformers and the Irish began well. The Patriote bookseller, Hector Fabre, subsidized the Montreal *Vindicator*, edited by Dr. Daniel Tracey.[41] In the town of York, Francis Collins, the Irish editor of the *Canadian Freeman*,[42] was jailed for libel against the ruling party, the

"Family Compact". But this emerging alliance was arrested by the flood of immigration which inundated the Canadian provinces between 1828 and 1832.

As early as 1830, Ogle Robert Gowan, who had arrived in 1829 and organized the first Orange Grand Lodge in Canada at the end of the year, attempted to run for the local assembly in Upper Canada as the immigrant candidate. Gowan declared that as one-third of the inhabitants of Leeds County were Irish, one of the three candidates elected should be an Irishman.[43] Two years later, Dr. Tracey, running in a by-election in Montreal that ended in a riot with troops firing on the electors,[44] made the same appeal, declaring the Irish of Montreal to be one-third of the population. Both Gowan, who ran as an independent, and Tracey, who ran as a Reformer, recognized a distinct immigrant interest, and both appealed to all Irishmen without regard to religion. Gowan, although titular head of the Canadian Orangemen, who had since 1824 battled annually with Catholics on July 12th, perceived that the common interest of the Irish as outsiders in the New World took precedence over the historic quarrels of the Orange and the Green.

What Tracey and his successor, Dr. Edmund Bayley O'Callaghan, did not perceive was that the Catholic-Liberal alliance formed by O'Connell in Ireland was based on a common opposition to an Anglican church establishment which, in spite of the clergy reserves, had no real substance in Canada. Although the Irish Catholics might assume that their natural enemies in the New World would be British officialdom and its Tory and Orange supporters, this assumption was soon tempered by the popular prejudice against immigrants held by natives and settlers of long residence upon whom the Reform movements were based.

The divergence between the Irish and the Reformers came with the immigrant head tax, a government measure supported by the Reformers. This measure could be defended on the grounds of the general good, but immigrants considered it an injury, and its passage was accompanied by attacks on "pauper" immigration which Irish immigrants in particular regarded as insults to themselves. Yet William Lyon Mackenzie tried to secure Irish support through an alliance with the rector of York, Father William O'Grady, who was challenging the authority of Bishop Alexander Macdonell. Mackenzie's incautious intervention in Catholic affairs led to a union of Irish and Tories in the York riots of 1832 during which Mackenzie was roughly handled. He retaliated by joining in the attacks on Irish pauper immigration.[45]

Edmund B. O'Callaghan continued to support the Patriote party of Papineau in the columns of the Montreal *Vindicator*. O'Callaghan was elected to the provincial assembly for the French Canadian constituency of Yamaska, becoming one of the principal leaders of the Reform party in Lower Canada, but he lost his influence among the Montreal Irish.[46] With the founding in 1835 of a second Irish newspaper in Montreal, the *Irish Advocate,* which was edited by the Limerick-born Montreal lawyer, John Ponsonby Sexton, the Montreal Irish rallied to the government.[47]

In the crucial Upper Canadian election of 1836, part of Gowan's design was realized when the Orange and Catholic vote was united in support of the loyalist coalition under the Lieutenant Governor, Sir Francis Bond Head. Irish volunteers filled the ranks of the loyalist militia in both provinces on the eve of the abortive rebellions of 1837, their enthusiasm being noted by loyalist John Beverley Robinson and by Mackenzie himself. Head urged the appointment of Irishman Peter de Blaquière to the Legislative Council "even though he has only recently arrived in the Province" as the "Irish have complained and with reason that they have been neglected."[48]

The Catholic question had yet to become a serious issue in the Canadian provinces, being manifest only in quarrels among the immigrant population rather than quarrels between natives and immigrants. French Canadian Catholic bishops had opposed the uprisings in Lower Canada at considerable cost to their popularity, and Daniel O'Connell, whose followers in the House of Commons supported the British government, also condemned the Canadian rebellions.[49] In the United States, the Irish American community sympathized as a matter of course with any rebellion against British authority, but as the

Canadian rebellions did not coincide with a similar movement in Ireland, they were at first not much concerned with
Canadian affairs. With the organization of the Hunters Lodges
in 1838 by Canadian exiles and their American sympathizers,
however, the Canadian rebellions became an American
concern.

The Hunters anticipated the Fenians, organizing raids in
the same border areas and creating similar problems for Canadian and American authorities. Unlike the Fenians, the Hunters were based on native, or at least assimilated sections, of the
American population living within easy access of the frontier,
rather than on an immigrant population concentrated in large
cities. The Hunters had the advantage of being linked to an
extensive underground network in French Canada and might
claim the sympathy of a substantial, if not very active, minority
in Upper Canada. Yet the Hunters could not, like the Fenians
after the American Civil War, draw on a vast reserve of dis-
banded soldiers, but had to rely on the miscellaneous military
talents of the frontier population, for the most part trained
fighters rather than trained soldiers who looked on Canada as
the Texas of the north.[50]

The Hunters probably had about 80,000 or so sympathizers,
mostly Protestant Americans. They were supported by a substantial section of the press in the border regions whose enthusiasm for Americanization of the continent was combined
with a zeal for temperance and abolitionism that was noticeable in anti-Catholic publications.[51] Yet there were no visible
links between a Protestant and a republican crusade. The col-
lector of customs at Oswego reported to American authorities
at Washington that "No small number of the middle class,
comprehending many persons of enterprize, industry and pro-
perty, are engaged in the movement." To this body of substantial citizens were added professional crusaders like the
Pole, N. S. von Schoultz, and C. G. Bryant, a former servant of
the republic of Texas.[52]

While moral and financial support might be provided by
substantial citizens, and leadership found among political crusaders, the ranks of the Hunters were recruited largely from

the unemployed and more adventurous elements along the
border — two categories that included many Irishmen. Such
Irishmen, particularly if they had been Ribbonmen, would feel
at home in lodges where an oath was administered to blind-
folded, kneeling candidates, and which had varying degrees
such as the Snowshoe, Beaver, Master Hunter, and Patriot
Hunter. Although in theory crusaders for democracy, the
Hunters were not organized democratically, as the higher
military ranks were reserved for those holding higher degrees
within the lodges. Hunters claimed that they enforced secrecy
with the death penalty, thereby providing prime examples of
the conspiratorial associations so much deplored by the anti-
Masonic party and the anti-Catholic journalists.[53]

An obvious link between the Irish and the Hunters, Edmund
O'Callaghan, was lost to the movement because he, like Papineau, rejected the plans for raids across the Canadian border
from the United States. But the Irish presence in the Hunters
was represented by E. A. Theller, an Irish immigrant who,
after living for a time in Montreal, had settled in Detroit.
Theller was commissioned as a brigadier general in the "Patriot Army" with orders to recruit Irish and French volunteers
in Upper Canada. He was captured in 1838, tried, convicted
of treason, and condemned to death. According to his own
account, he brought tears to the eyes of the Irish loyalist volunteers when he spoke during his trial of the wrongs of Ireland.[54]
More pointedly, he raised the question of whether a naturalized American citizen could be tried for treason against the
British Crown. Theller's sentence was suspended indefinitely,
but while he was being held at Quebec City for transfer to
England he escaped from custody and returned to the United
States. In New York, he was given a public dinner which was
presided over by Dr. William James MacNeven, the last prominent survivor of the United Irishmen. However, the Bishop of
New York did not attend and Theller, in his account of the
proceedings, makes no mention of clergy being present. Theller
was similarly welcomed in Philadelphia by the Irish community, but in Washington, D. C., and Baltimore, his reception by the Irish ran into official hostility. Public buildings

were not available and leading newspapers refused to print notices of the meetings.[55]

The Hunters had at first enjoyed considerable sympathy among Americans, particularly after the Canadian militia had burned the Hunter supply ship, the *Caroline,* in American waters. They even received some official patronage from senators and governors of the border states who, having no direct responsibility for foreign policy, could afford to indulge their sympathies and could not ignore Hunter influence on the local electorate.

Yet, as in the days of the United Irishmen in the 1790s, the federal government was not prepared to let sympathies with a foreign rebellion jeopardize American relations with Great Britain. The Hunters, when faced with federal measures to enforce the neutrality laws, did not hesitate to attack the Van Buren administration which they had at first hoped to win over. William Lyon Mackenzie, who was at this time seeking a place in American politics, was delighted to add the voice of his Rochester *Gazette* to those American journals which blamed the depression of 1837 on British banks, and he saw President Van Buren as an agent of British finance. Canadians resident in the United States were urged to turn in their bank notes and demand gold and silver as a means of defeating British influence.[56] Mackenzie also courted the Irish community by printing Irish news, and articles on Irish history. He was rewarded by being placed twelfth in a list of thirteen heroes and celebrities being toasted at St. Patrick's Day dinners in 1840. General Richard Montgomery, who had tried to storm Quebec, was tenth, Canada was eleventh, while the final toast was reserved for the "fair sex".[57]

By the time Theller reached Washington, the Hunters were being closely watched by federal authorities, but they still hoped to provoke a war between the United States and Great Britain. They even attempted to profit by current tensions between Russia and Britain by making contact with the Russian consul in New York.[58] The final effort of the Hunters was designed to disrupt the negotiations which led to the signing of the Webster-Ashburton Treaty. They spread rumours that they

were preparing raids along the frontier, but these rumours
were dispelled easily when the Montreal chief of police toured
the border area,[59] and the treaty was signed in 1842.

## O'CONNELL'S REPEAL CAMPAIGN

During the days of the Hunters, the fall of the Melbourne
government in Britain left O'Connell in the opposition and
free to resume his campaign for the repeal of the parliamentary union between Britain and Ireland. It was evident that
this movement would cross the Atlantic and provide an outlet
for the same kind of crusading zeal that had influenced the
supporters of the Hunters Lodges. In the autumn of 1841,
Father T. A. Pulby, the parish priest of Paterson, New Jersey,
wrote that the Hunters were uniting with Repeal Associations
and complained that, "As I would not permit a Repeal Association to be established in this town, I was made to understand that my love of Ireland, if not my faith as a Catholic,
was doubted".[60]
    Yet the Repeal Association represented the spirit of consti-
tutionalism which never went beyond turbulent mass meetings
and provided little scope for the conspiratorial talents of the
Hunters. The main work of the North American Repealers
was to raise money for the cause of repeal and consequently
they needed the support of loyalist Canadians as well as the
adherents of the administrations of Van Buren and his successor, President John Tyler, who had enforced the neutrality
legislation.
    The Repealers were able to attract leading Canadian Re-
formers, but their most useful recruit was Robert Tyler, the
son of the American president who joined the Repeal Association in 1843 and presided over the Repeal Convention in New
York City in 1844. These loyal Repeal Associations were rea-
sonably successful in raising money. Some $10,000 was sent to
Ireland from Boston in 1844, but their real importance was
that they provided Irish Americans with a sense of taking part
in contemporary Irish politics.[61] Like their predecessor, the

Friends of Ireland, they represented the migration of the spirit of Irish constitutionalism to North America, which offered an alternative to the conspiratorial and republican traditions of the United Irishmen.

As in the case of the Friends of Ireland, the Repealers did not arouse a fear of conspiracy or create international incidents, but, as they assembled large numbers of Irishmen for political purposes, they must be counted among the causes of the outbreak of nativism in the 1840s. The underlying cause was, perhaps, the presence of increasingly more immigrants than American society could hope to assimilate. Of these, the most conspicuous group was Irish. To this must be added the assumption of many Protestants that the Catholic church was not only a barrier to assimilation but the ultimate cause of poverty, drunkenness, and riotous conduct of the immigrants.

This feeling was undoubtedly strengthened by the strong stand that Bishop John Hughes of New York took against Bible reading in public schools in the early 1840s. At this time the main centres of nativist propaganda were New York and Philadelphia. Here tension boiled over in May and June of 1844 when Protestant demonstrators, marching provocatively through Catholic districts, were fired on. Protestant mobs retaliated by burning two Catholic churches and several blocks of Irish dwellings. The Bishop of Philadelphia ordered Catholics to keep clear of Protestant demonstrators and closed the churches on the Sunday following the first serious outbreaks.[62] In New York, Bishop Hughes declared that the Catholics of Philadelphia were wrong in not defending their churches and he warned that New York would become a second Moscow if one church was burned.[63] A force of from one to two thousand would be required, he announced, to protect each church. This stand appears to have frightened nativist groups in New York who cancelled a public meeting at which a delegation from Philadelphia was to address an assembly in Central Park.[64]

As in the case of the burning of the Ursuline convent in Boston ten years before, violence tended to produce a momentary reaction against nativism. Moreover, public attention was soon distracted from the Irish to the war with Mexico. Yet this war against a Catholic power provided opportunities for anti-Catholic propaganda. Catholic soldiers in the American forces were compelled to attend Protestant church parades and there were protests against the appointment of Catholic chaplains in the United States armed forces.[65] This treatment may explain the relative ease with which Irish deserters were recruited into the San Patrico Brigade which served with distinction in the Mexican forces. Moreover, the hanging of soldiers of the San Patrico Brigade after the fall of Mexico City added to the resentments of the Irish Americans.[66]

By the end of the Mexican war, Irish nationalism had become part of the culture and politics of the Irish Americans. The settlements of Irish in neighbourhoods and districts, the continuous stream of immigrants, and trans-Atlantic family connections made it clear that Irish nationalism would remain so for several generations. Although there were still Protestant nationalists among the survivors of 1798, and among O'Connellite journalists, the Irish Americans had become a Catholic community and their most important institution was the church. In the half-century after the rising of 1798, the influence of O'Connellism had displaced the early republican organizations. There remained a republican tradition which was woven into the general pattern of Irish folklore but lacked a surviving republican organization.

The emergence of O'Connellite organizations in North America demonstrated the ability of the Irish overseas to provide moral and financial support for nationalism in Ireland. It remained for the shock of the Irish famine, which brought about a sudden and vast expansion of the Irish population in North America and a revival of republicanism in Ireland, to prepare the way for the organization of the Fenian Brotherhood.

# CHAPTER TWO

# Genesis of Fenianism

While the small United Irish organization in America was intended to be an auxiliary to the movement already established in Ireland, the Fenian Brotherhood was created on the initiative of Irish Americans who remained equal, if not senior, partners in the trans-Atlantic organization. This shift in balance was primarily the result of the mass exodus of the Irish after the potato famine of 1845, an exodus that would, in time, create an Irish population overseas exceeding that of the Irish at home.

Although the Irish (and with them, Irish political traditions) migrated to Britain, Canada, and other future dominions of the British Empire, the vast majority went to the United States, and it was only on American soil that a republican conspiracy against the established government in Ireland could be organized openly. Annual immigration to the United States rose to 100,000 in 1845, 300,000 in 1850, and reached its peak of 427,833 in 1854. Much of this immigration was German, but German peasants settling on farms in the Midwest were less of a social irritant than the Irish who crowded into the northeastern cities. By 1860, in New York and Boston, the foreign-born out-numbered the natives, and by 1850 there were 4,000,000 of Irish background out of a total population of 24,000,000.[1]

The arrival of 500,000 Irish in New York City between 1845 and 1850[2] vastly increased the responsibilities of Bishop John Hughes, who was made Archbishop of New York in 1850. This growth of immigrant numbers and the consequent expansion of the Roman Catholic church almost inevitably led to a "nativist" and anti-Catholic reaction which emerged as the "Know-Nothing" movement in the early fifties. Taking the name of "American party", this group elected governors in four New England states, and in Maryland, Kentucky, and California.[3]

In the face of this organized hostility, it was difficult for Irish republicans in America to present the American system as an ideal for Ireland. Yet this is what they did and had to do. In the strange and somewhat hostile American environment, the Irish would look back to the familiar pattern of Irish politics, welcoming the sense of participating in the politics of Ireland which Irish American nationalists could give them. Moreover, there was much in contemporary Irish politics to capture the imagination of the immigrant population.

In the course of the nineteenth century, a new dimension had been added to Irish nationalism under the influence of the Romantic movement. The younger followers of O'Connell had sought to assert the historic existence of Ireland by a revival of interest in Celtic folklore, Jacobite traditions, and the United Irishmen of 1798. This movement was especially attractive to the Irish overseas whose feelings for Ireland could not easily be sustained without literary support. Poems, articles, and books dealing with Irish themes were supplemented by night classes and public lectures such as those given by Thomas D'Arcy McGee when, at the age of seventeen, he toured New England in 1843 as the representative of the Boston *Pilot*. By presenting Irish history and literature in an attractive and exciting manner, he, like other Irish intellectuals, diffused in the American mind and to some extent in the European mind an awareness of Ireland's historic grievances.[4]

Leading this literary movement was the *Nation*, a journal published in Dublin, which attracted a circulation of 10,000, a very large one for that time. The talents of D'Arcy McGee were soon recognized by Gavan Duffy, editor of the *Nation*, who invited McGee to join its staff and McGee subsequently became part of the "Young Ireland" group which had become impatient with O'Connell's leadership. At first, this group demanded a more aggressive pursuit of the policy of mass agitation and did not attract the attention of the Irish Americans. It was not until O'Connell's death in 1847 that the Young Irelanders came under the influence of the republican revival in Europe and, with the success of the French Revolution of February 1848, were converted to the idea of a barricade revolution carried out by a citizen militia. Taking the name of "Confederates", they conspired to re-enact the French Revolution on Irish soil. These Young Irelanders were more attracted by the romance of revolution than by the republican form of government, and only one of their leaders, James Fintan Lalor, considered the possibility of social revolution.[5]

As literary men with no experience in the art of conspiracy, they were at best amateur revolutionaries. Theirs was essentially open conspiracy, with a reliance on the diffusion of military knowledge, rifle clubs, the belief in a spontaneous uprising of the peasantry, and a hope of defection among Crown forces to the expected popular movement. An Irish uprising seemed to follow logically from the waves of revolutions sweeping Europe. When Irish crowds showed a preference for republican over O'Connellite oratory, it was easy to assume that they were prepared for barricades. The willingness of Irishmen to join illegal organizations and to engage in illegal activity provided further encouragement.

Yet there was little enthusiasm for the kind of risk and sacrifices needed to support an uprising and what there was could not be efficiently organized by amateur revolutionaries. They were easily out-manoeuvred by the government, which soon discovered the plans for the rising and arrested the leaders before their plans matured. As it was impossible to challenge the alerted garrisons in the large cities, the Confederates fell back on efforts to raise the countryside. These expired amid peasant indifference.

Yet literary men have the ability to write themselves into history. The near bloodless and often ludicrous episodes of their rising were presented and to a large degree accepted as tragedy. Although there were no executions, some leaders lived for a while under sentence of death. Others were exiled to Australia and still others escaped to America or France. The rising provided an abundance of dramatic courtroom scenes and hairbreadth escapes, the stuff of folklore rather than history. The romance of these episodes understandably captured the imagination of the Irish Americans who eagerly awaited news of the rising and, after its failure, the arrival of the exiles.

Moreover, for the first time since the days of the United Irishmen, there was a republican movement in Ireland which might claim the sympathies of republican America, which had recently been triumphant in the war with Mexico and still more recently had been engaged in a dispute with Britain concerning the future of the Oregon territory. Like the United Irishmen, the Young Irelanders sent emissaries to revolutionary republicans in France and, if they could not deal directly with the government of the United States, they might have hoped to exert influence through the Irish Americans. If the old order was crumbling in Europe, could the United States hesitate to destroy the old order in North America as represented by the British American provinces?

In the spring of 1848, a Young Ireland emissary, Thomas Francis Meagher, was arrested on the eve of his departure for America. He was replaced by John Mitchel, who was welcomed with enthusiasm by the Irish American veterans of the Mexican war who offered their services to the Irish conspirators. Some $40,000 was collected with little difficulty. A military club, the Irish Republican Union, which had been founded before Mitchel's arrival, directed its attention towards Canada.[6]

Yet there could be no popular crusade on behalf of Irish nationalism in America, and there was at the most only regional interest in the annexation of Canada because of the reluctance of the southern states to have free territory added to the Union. Nor were the Irish republicans capable of launching a raid across the frontier at this time. But it was possible to hold public meetings and to make threats amid the prevailing tension. Perhaps it was fitting that what was in many respects a mock revolution should be supported in North America by a mock invasion of Canada.

The Canadian provinces were at this time undergoing an economic crisis and the newly elected La Fontaine—Baldwin administration had yet to demonstrate its capacity for leadership. In the spring of 1848 the unrest which was to culminate in the Annexation Manifesto of 1849 was already maturing. Merchant classes had been alienated by the repeal of the Corn Laws. Papineau, recently returned from exile, contemplated a future for French Canada as "La Petite Louisiana du Nord". The Irish Republican Union could hardly harness such unrest, yet the unrest provided evidence which might be used to convince American audiences that Canadians would welcome annexation.

Against this background, the Canadian governor, Lord Elgin, had to interpret rumours of Irish republican conspiracies. Elgin wrote on April 22, 1848 that "A secret combination of Irish in Montreal is on foot, and bound together by oaths, having designs inimical to the Government; that the number enrolled is at least 17,000 and that they look to the acquisition of arms and gun powder stored on St. Helen's Island."[7] Later he noted that of his twelve ministers, four were Irish born, one—Baldwin—was of Irish parents, four were French Canadians, and only three were of English or Scots origin. Elgin elaborated:

I hope that we shall have no trouble from the other side—I am inclined however to believe that the Hunters Lodges (secret societies of sympathizers) are organized—and that if an outbreak takes place in Ireland, there may be a desire among the Irish to effect a diversion in favor of their Countrymen by exciting disturbances here. . . . How are we prepared to meet the difficulty? . . . The Ministers and their supporters are, I think, staunch; so also, is the body of Tories of Upper Canada. . . . Among the mercantile classes, now that protection is abandoned . . . and the

old conservative hangers out of office, . . . now that Responsible
Govt. is fairly carried out, much indifference as to the maintenance
or surrender of the connexion with Great Britain will, I fear, be
found. Papineau and his adherents and a certain class of Irish
are of course ready for anything that will create confusion without
much heed as to what may follow. So much for our morale.[8]

Elgin found no further cause for alarm until he received a
placard dated appropriately July 4, announcing "A Prepara-
tory Meeting of the Friends of Ireland will be held at
McAuley's Hotel, opposite the Bonsecours Market, on
Thursday, the 6th inst., at eight o'clock, to make arrange-
ments for the Receipt of the Brother of the Martyred Mitchel
and the Delegate from the New York Republican Union; also
to take means for convening a Monster Meeting!" The placard
went on, "Men of Ireland! The Day is fast approaching
when your suffering country's fate shall be decided! You
know your duty!! Fear not!! Your cause is good, and it will
prosper if you will only prove yourselves faithful and true."[9]

Elgin received a visit from an "MPP opposed in politics to
the present local government", who told him that there was
a popular movement being organized in the United States
with designs to organize from "700,000 to 800,000 men under
an American general lately returned from Mexico", and that
"fifty thousand Irish were already prepared to march". The
MPP's source of information was Michael Thomas O'Connor,
who was to address a mass meeting at Bonsecours Market.[10]

Under pressure from the governor, the mayor of Montreal,
Joseph Bourret, denied the use of the Market to the Irish and
the meeting was held in the open at Haymarket Square
instead. Several hundred assembled to hear addresses by
Bernard Devlin and Sydney Bellingham, two prominent
Montreal lawyers. The secretary read a message from Benjamin
Holmes, a prominent liberal politician and leader of the
Irish community who told them that the meeting could do
nothing for Ireland and would retard the cause of good government in Canada. O'Connor's speech was interrupted by
rain and the crowd retired to McAuley's Hotel. Elgin con-

templated taking legal action against O'Connor,[11] but he was
not sure that he had sufficient evidence for an indictment.

In spite of this somewhat disappointing gathering, O'Connor
reported to a meeting in New York two weeks later that he
had addressed a crowd of 6,000 republicans in Montreal and
"that everyone with whom he had come in contact told him
that they looked forward with pleasure to the happy day when
their country should become part and parcel of the United
States." He also told his audience that on meeting fifty men
of the 19th Regiment "every man took off his cap to him as
he passed". He assured his listeners that of the 10,000 British
regulars in Canada, not 3,000 would fight for England.

O'Connor then gave an account of the Canadian rebellion
of 1837, declaring that "it is not generally known that the
late Canadian Revolution was put down by Irishmen in
Canada and by the cowardly conduct of Van Buren [president
of the United States]." This presumably could not happen
again. O'Connor asserted, "The Lion of England's whelps
should be lashed . . . . Canada must be invaded. She herself
loudly demands it. She has no commerce, no trade, 2,000
shops were to be let in the City of Montreal, wages had
lowered 50% and no man could live in comfort."[12]

O'Connor's comments on the economic crisis, although
exaggerated, had some foundation as the repeal of the English
Corn Laws in 1846 had been damaging to Canadian commerce. Elgin was at that moment attempting to redress the
balance by seeking concessions for Canadian produce in
American markets through a reciprocity treaty. The comment
about the loyalty of the 19th Regiment cannot be taken
seriously as the regiment had been confined to barracks on the
day O'Connor allegedly exchanged greetings with fifty of its
men on Notre Dame Street.[13]

Although the activity of the Irish Republican Union was
merely a question of threats, the threats continued throughout
the summer and could not be ignored. On August 16, Elgin
wrote that, "The news from Ireland—the determination of
Govt not to proceed with the measure respecting the Naviga-
tion Laws, doubts as to whether the American Congress will
pass the reciprocity of trade Bill, menaces of sympathizers in

the States—all combine at present to render our position one of considerable anxiety . . . . We have the Irish repeal Body—I need not describe them—You may look at home— they are here just what they are in Ireland."[14]

Elgin then went on to give his account of the French Canadians. "Their attitude," he wrote, "as regards England and America is that of an armed neutrality—They do not exactly like the Yankees but they are the *conquered oppressed subjects* of England.—To be sure they govern themselves, get all the places, pay no taxes, and some other trifles of this description—Nevertheless, they are the victims of British Egoisme. Was not the union of the Provinces carried without their consent and with the view of subjecting them to the British? Papineau, their press and other authorities, are constantly dinning this into their ears, so no wonder that they believe it."[15]

With regard to external aggression, Elgin declared, "I shall throw the responsibility of repelling them upon Her Majesty's troops in the first instance. This is the service wh [*sic*] we profess to render to our Colonies without charge to them. It is well that they should see this benefit resulting from the connexion, and I shall be disappointed indeed if the military here do not give a very good acct [*sic*] of all Yankee and Irish marauders notwithstanding the swagger of the cutthroats from Mexico."[16]

Elgin had reports from R. B. Sullivan, the provincial secretary who had visited the United States, and from Crampton, the British minister in Washington.[17] Sullivan considered that the Mexican victory and the presidential election had stimulated a dangerous spirit of aggression among Americans. Crampton doubted the capacity of the Irish to organize effective aggression but even he was worried that during the coming winter, when the Irish had little employment, they would combine with ex-soldiers to create difficulties.

With the collapse of the rebellion in Ireland in 1848, the activities of the Irish Republican Union faded away. By November 16, Elgin was able to write, "I hear every now and then of emissaries from the New York Irish confederates, and I have reason to believe that gentry of this class are dropping in among us occasionally—but I hardly think they can have anything very serious in hand at present."[18]

In Ireland itself, republicanism underwent a second eclipse and within two years the leading Irish churchman, Archbishop Paul Cullen, the future cardinal, gave his support to a revived constitutionalism in the form of the "Irish Independent party". Gavan Duffy, who had been tried and acquitted of treason in 1848, supported the new party which was referred to by British parliamentarians as the "Pope's Brass Band".[19] Republicanism in Ireland was limited to scattered discussion groups such as the Phoenix Society which met in Skibbereen and seemed destined to go the way of the United Irishmen.

There remained the exiles, but the leaders of the Young Ireland movement, although temporarily fascinated by the romance of revolution, were not prepared to become professional revolutionaries. Like the exiled United Irishmen, they tended to follow more conventional careers as lawyers, journalists, and politicians in their adopted country. This set limits to the time and energy which they could devote to revolutionary enterprise.

Among the first exiles to arrive in America was young Thomas D'Arcy McGee, carrying with him the prestige of having taken part in the rising. This gave him a temporary advantage over the established Irish republicans such as the publishers of the *Irish American* who immediately had to face the competition of McGee's New York *Nation*. McGee brought with him the authorized republican explanation for failure. Risings in the cities had been impossible because of the strength of the garrison. Risings in the countryside had been defeated by the influence of the clergy. This explanation was understandably rejected by the church and particularly by Bishop John Hughes of New York who had sympathized with the Young Ireland movement before the rising. Hughes had no hesitation in responding, as did most of the hierarchy, that revolt had been undertaken without popular support and that the ineptitude of the leaders was itself sufficient explanation for defeat.[20]

McGee at this time was a champion of international revolution. He found the Pope in his capacity as a temporal prince to be an ally of continental despotism, and on these grounds McGee justified Garibaldi's occupation of Rome. In McGee's view, there were two great camps—the czars and the dynasties on one side, and the press, burghers, and students on the other. The Pope had taken the wrong side, but America, he hoped, might yet become "God's worthy instrument for liberating Europe".[21]

As a British colony, Canada was presumed to be oppressed and seeking emancipation. McGee emphatically rejected the idea that the recent grant of responsible government had altered the colonial status of the province and, in support of his view, he might have found some encouragement in the emergence of the Annexation movement in 1849. In an appeal to Irish Canadians, he wrote, "The politics of your Colony have assumed a character which attracts the attention and excites hope in the Irish race—the question of your independence from Britain . . . the common oppressor of our native and adopted countries . . . we look to you to protect yourselves and avenge the famines of '46, '47, and '48 and their heartless authors." Yet McGee urged caution: "We do not counsel you to originate a Revolution. . . . But if a struggle must come in Canada, we exhort you to be prepared, to act a prompt and powerful part, worthy of your numbers and your race. . . . Cultivate the confidence and love of your French neighbours. Remember the ancient friendship of France and Ireland. Teach the habitants to regard republicans as their friends, learn to make them such in reality."[22] In spite of his warning against taking the initiative, McGee ended his exhortation to Irish Canadians by declaring, "Canada never had a better opportunity. India is involved with the Sikhs, Ireland is thoroughly disloyal and thoroughly desperate."[23]

Encouragement of this kind was extended as a matter of course to rebels everywhere, but particularly to those likely to oppose British rule. Behind this encouragement, as far as Canada was concerned, were the potentialities of the Irish American military clubs which by 1849 were finding their way into the militia of various states. There had always been

Irish companies such as the Columbian Company of Artillery in Boston.[24] This unit included Irish nationalists but, unlike the Irish Republican Union which became at this point the 9th Regiment of the New York National Guard, the Columbian Company of Artillery was not organized and dominated by avowed Irish republicans. Like the 9th Regiment, the 69th Regiment of the New York National Guard, which was raised in the 1850s and later became known as the "Fighting 69th",[25] was an Irish republican unit. These volunteer corps, with their distinctive uniforms and brass bands, were ideally suited to the needs of those who hoped to create the nucleus of an Irish army in America.

Writing in 1850, McGee noted with pride that there were in the United States twenty-five or thirty Irish companies of militia, and he estimated the total number of Irish Americans with military training at 50,000. The Irish, he insisted, "should cultivate the military arts, which stood high among the republican virtues . . . . [They should] revive the taste for tactics and apply themselves to the study of military science."

McGee first appears in America as another republican crusader, perhaps a worthy successor of Wolfe Tone. Yet he could not succeed in New York in the face of the competition of established journalists and the hostility of Bishop John Hughes. In 1850 he moved to the more congenial atmosphere of Boston where, with the encouragement of Bishop James Fitzpatrick, a distant relative, he edited the *American Celt*. McGee had already tempered his republicanism by a concern for the condition of Irish immigrants in America and by degrees he moved away from the anti-clericalism of his first years in America. By 1852 he was writing of the "most dangerous and general conspiracies against Christendom"[26] and he warned Catholics that they must resist "The conspirators who, under the stolen name of Liberty, make war upon all Christian institutions."[27] In the same year, McGee, having offended the anti-clerical Irish in Boston and seeing no opportunity there for his increasingly conservative journal, moved the *American Celt* to Buffalo.

McGee's journal did not flourish in Buffalo, even with the useful and interesting contacts he made with Canadians, and

in 1854 he returned to New York. Here the arrival of the
Young Irelanders from the penal colony in Australia set the
stage for quarrels among the exiles, quarrels which McGee
could hardly hope to avoid. The escape of the exiles from
Australia had been arranged by the Irish Republican Directory, an agency created for the purpose of aiding political
prisoners. This proved to be the most impressive of the exile
institutions, as money and sympathy could more easily be
found for political prisoners than for conspiracy. Included
among the directors was the formidable editor of the New
York *Tribune*, Horace Greeley.

Among the exiles to arrive in the United States was John
Mitchel, who reached New York late in 1853 and announced
his intention of founding a new nationalist newspaper, the
*Citizen*.[28] In the pattern of D'Arcy McGee in 1848, Mitchel
quarrelled with the church and the other Irish nationalists.
Mitchel, who was of Presbyterian background, wrote that the
hierarchy of the church "is the enemy of Irishmen [which]
twice, in '98 and '48 delivered over the Catholic people of
Ireland . . . . The Irish here will be good and loyal people
of the Republic in the exact proportion that they cut themselves off, not from Religion, but from the Political Corpora-
tion which you call the Church of God."[29]

In spite of this strong language and his quarrels with other
nationalists, Mitchel might have survived as a journalist had
he not compounded his difficulties by a defence of slavery and
attacks on the abolitionist leader, Henry Ward Beecher.
Before the end of 1854, he found it expedient to retire to
Knoxville, Tennessee, but before leaving he had time enough
to participate in the work which led to the founding of the
Fenian organization three years later.

Mitchel regarded the outbreak of the Crimean War as
Ireland's opportunity. On April 13, 1854 he founded the
Irishman's Civil and Military Republican Union which, unlike
existing military clubs, was intended to prepare for the
imminent liberation of Ireland. Mitchel contacted the Russian
consul in New York to secure assistance,[30] but with his abrupt
departure for the South, the lead was taken by two other
exiles, John O'Mahony and Michael Doheny. Doheny, a

former "confederate" who had become a successful lawyer, organized the Emmet Monument Society early in 1855. The new society was to justify the erection of a monument to Emmet by winning independence, for Emmet had asked before his execution in 1801 that no monument be raised to him until Ireland had secured independence. O'Mahony, who had been in Paris until 1850, took up negotiations with the Russians in the hope of securing transport to Ireland for 2,000 men and arms for 5,000 more.[31]

The absence of an organization in Ireland presented obvious difficulties, but the best that could be done was to authorize Joseph Denieffe, who was going to Ireland on private business, to spread rumours of a landing in the autumn of 1855.[32] Divisions among Irish American nationalists led Doheny to found a newspaper of his own, the *Honest Truth*, and then to create a second republican organization. This involved calling an Irish American convention of representatives from local public meetings. The representatives would then select a directory to act as a provisional government for Ireland. A step towards effecting this was taken when the Massachusetts Emigrant Aid Society was formed in Boston on August 14, 1855 to provide aid to emigrants returning to "liberate" Ireland.[33]

Neither this society nor the Emmet Monument Society survived the end of the Crimean War in 1856 and neither evoked much sympathy from the American press. Yet the essence of Fenianism was to be found in the idea of a military club engaged in the preparation for immediate action and the idea of a "government in exile". The missing element was a secret organization in Ireland itself.

A second convention of a different kind was organized by D'Arcy McGee in Buffalo in January 1856. Its purpose was to encourage and subsidize the movement of Irish Americans from the Eastern cities to agricultural settlements in the West.[34] These conventions represented opposite tendencies among Irish Americans. For those who met in Boston, as well as for O'Mahony and Mitchel, the survival of the Irish as a nationality demanded the establishment of an independent state, linked to America by a common republicanism. Ireland

once free, would become an America in Europe. For D'Arcy
McGee, whose views were respected, if not shared, by the
hierarchy of the church, the danger was that in the Protestant
and secular environment of republican America, the Irish
might lose their religion and sense of nationality. The poverty
of the cities, McGee found, loosened family ties, and urban
politics, personified by Tammany Hall, were a demoralizing
influence. Exile politics were wrong, he insisted, if only because they were futile.[35]

McGee's altered view of America was strengthened by the
resurgence of nativism and anti-Catholicism in the form of the
Know-Nothing party. Republicanism had proved a mixed
blessing for Irishmen in the New World and he had doubts
about the advantages of introducing it in Ireland. The solu-
tion for Irish Americans, in his view, was to move out of the
cities into new land in the West, and this, coupled with his
attitude towards republican ideology, led him to a favourable
view of Canada.

In the spring of 1855, McGee felt able to write that Irishmen
planning to emigrate to America should be informed of the
advantages of settling in Canada. "The British provinces of
North America are not necessarily miserable and uninhabit-
able because the British flag flies at Quebec. That flag, without
feudal landlordism, without a national debt, without a state
church, is shorn of its worst terrors . . . . To a Country like
Canada, a federal connection [with Great Britain] and an Imperial flag is the best foreign alliance and best guarantee of
peaceful progress, under a parliament of her own election."
McGee also noted that the population was less hostile to Catholics and that parents could more effectively supervise the education of their children".[36]

Such views, expressed in New York while the Irish republicans were engaged in military preparations, posed a challenge
to the "myth" which was essential to the purposes of the Irish
republicans. It was necessary for them to contrast the condition
of servitude of the Irish under the British flag with the freedom and well-being under republican institutions in America.
It was not surprising that the *Citizen* accused McGee of preparing a "stampede to Canada" and of "disparaging the insti-

tutions of the republic".[37] McGee replied that, "Under certain conditions which may unfortunately happen, I should not shrink under any degree of opposition from advising an Irish landslide out of a proselytizing state of society . . . such as we are threatened with in the republic . . . into a self-governing Province where religious freedom can still be enjoyed".[38]

McGee could hardly avoid comment on the military preparations then in progress. This provided him with an opportunity of making it clear that he "had given up the advocating of any special Irish-American organization". He added that the material for creating revolutionary movements among the Irish "always exists, [it] is found at an hour's notice in the generous hearts of our emigrants".[39] Instead of armed conspiracy, McGee recommended that aid to Ireland should be provided in the form of assistance to Catholic educational and charitable institutions.

The end of the Crimean War dissolved the hopes of the Irish republicans, and it became evident to the leaders of the defunct Emmet Monument Society that if they expected further public support, a movement in Ireland must somehow be created. Meanwhile, McGee's convention in Buffalo, although well attended, failed to arouse Irish American enthusiasm for westward migration. The following year, as though confirming the accusation of Mitchel, McGee accepted an invitation from the Irish Catholic community of Montreal to become its resident Irish intellectual. McGee and the Irish republicans would no longer be in direct conflict as McGee made his way in Canadian politics and the Irish Americans took the first steps towards organizing the Fenian Brotherhood.

JAMES STEPHENS AND JOHN O'MAHONY

Irish American nationalists could support an Irish revolutionary movement while remaining public figures in their own community, but in Ireland such a movement could only be organized by professional revolutionaries. And if young Irelanders were unwilling to assume this task, there were local leaders who attributed the failure of 1848 to the incompetence of the leaders and were prepared to try again. Among these were John O'Mahony and James Stephens who had lived among continental revolutionaries gathered in Paris, according to their own account, for the purpose of studying revolutionary techniques.

Stephens was the son of a Kilkenny auctioneer and bookseller. He had been baptized a Catholic, but had lived more among Protestants. An engineer by training, he took an active part in the fight at Ballingarry, the most serious skirmish during the rising of '48.[40] John O'Mahony was a gentleman farmer of Protestant background who was also active in '48. He had a keen interest in Celtic folklore and later developed an enthusiasm for spiritualism. Both men had potential as minor scholars and journalists. Stephens translated Dickens's *Martin Chuzzlewit* into French, and was praised by the author. O'Mahony, while in America, undertook to translate Keating's *History of Ireland* from Gaelic into English.[41]

In this respect, although less gifted, Stephens and O'Mahony resembled Duffy and McGee, but differed from them by their rejection of conventional politics. The rejection was complete in the case of Stephens who lived in hiding and worked in secret, while O'Mahony, whose primary task was to raise money, was a public figure, leading a voluntary organization, who had much in common with crusaders for other causes such as temperance and the abolition of slavery. While their taste for conspiracy was perhaps a matter of temperament, it was greatly strengthened by habits formed during their residence in Paris where they were, in theory at least, actively engaged in revolutionary conspiracy.

Stephens was to become a member of the International Workingman's Association which included Karl Marx,[42] and he preferred the company of continental revolutionaries to Irish Americans. Yet it seems that he was more interested in the methods of continental revolutionaries than in their ideas. It appears that he once considered Marshal MacMahon as a possible King of Ireland and wrote an anonymous pamphlet advocating a life presidency for a republican Ireland.

O'Mahony left Paris shortly after the end of the second French republic in 1852 and, as stated previously, became involved in Irish American politics, joining Michael Doheny and others in organizing the Emmet Monument Society. Stephens remained in Paris after O'Mahony's departure, preoccupied with translating, tutoring, and contributing to French journals until 1857. Then, in the spirit of an international revolutionary, he went to England with the idea of liberating Ireland by means of a republican revolution in Britain. He soon abandoned hope of this and undertook what he described as his 3,000 mile tour of Ireland, visiting veterans of '48 who often introduced him to local leaders of agrarian secret societies, or Ribbonmen. Stephens found younger Ribbon leaders more susceptible to his ideas, as were mechanics in the towns. However, he found the middle classes, including the veterans of '48, polite but hostile to the ideas of reviving the movement.[43]

Yet, conditions favourable to a new conspiratorial movement were maturing in Ireland. The Constitutionalists had lost the political initiative, and the Independent party no longer had the support of the church. One of its leading journalists, Frederick Lucas, had died, while Gavan Duffy had gone to Australia. The head of the Irish church, Archbishop Paul Cullen, was dissatisfied with all parties and offered no political leadership. It was at this juncture that the Irish republicans in New York decided to invite Stephens to found a new revolutionary movement in Ireland. Although the invitation was accompanied by a separate warning from O'Mahony that the offer came from men representing small and divided groups, Stephens's imagination was fired by the apparent potential of American financial and moral support. Stephens became a believer in the myth of American aid and it was this belief, more than the small sums of money and the handful of trained men sent from America, that sustained the movement in Ireland.

The expectation of substantial aid was as necessary to Stephens himself as it was to his followers in Ireland. Having accepted the myth, Stephens in a sense created a myth of his own which was essential to the existence of a large Irish republican movement in America — the myth of a powerful and well-organized underground army in Ireland, requiring only the material aid of Irish Americans to ensure its success.

This myth, too, had some substance. Stephens was able to

bring together a large number of local societies, some actually preparing for a rising. Fenianism was to be most successful in the cities, particularly in Dublin[44] itself where mechanics and shop assistants lived under conditions similar to those of the urbanized Irish Americans in the sense that they were sensitive to international political events. Moreover, they could easily assemble for public meetings and riots which provided them with a sense of taking part in high politics. There was also the excitement of clandestine meetings and of hiding fugitives, as well as other measures taken to evade the supervision of authorities. Apart from this, Fenianism would provide a means by which a feeling of social resentment could be expressed by attacks on the political order.

The military value of urban Fenians was questionable because of limited opportunities for training and the presence of the garrison in most cities. Stephens rested his hopes largely on the rural population, but here Fenian efforts were for the most part defeated by indifference on the part of the peasantry and by the hostility of the clergy. The Ribbon Societies were not prepared to make sacrifices for a movement led by intellectuals who promised a redress of grievances at some date which might be postponed indefinitely.

John O'Leary, the man who often served as Stephens's deputy, remarked that it was easier to make a rebel of an Orangeman than of a Ribbonman and that, in any event, peasants did not make good revolutionaries.[45] Yet Ireland was a peasant country and perhaps the most telling commentary on Fenian efforts among the peasantry was offered by Michael Davitt, one of the founders of the Land League. Davitt shrewdly observed that the landlords enjoyed a decade of peace while the Fenians were educating the "peasantry and working classes in the principles of Wolfe Tone and Emmet and in the lessons of independence taught by the poetry of Thomas Davis. . . . This, perhaps, accounts for the fact that from the year 1858 to that of 1870, these same landlords succeeded in evicting close upon 15,000 families from home and holdings."[46]

The Fenians, as Davitt suggested, may have distracted the peasantry from social protest, but Fenian influence fell far short of the power acquired by the United Irishmen in 1798.

Stephens could be bold and even reckless in carrying out schemes for training and recruiting, but he had a reluctance to commit his forces to action, which suggests a want of confidence in their strength and determination. Yet Stephens was a magnetic personality, ably assisted by his second-in-command, Thomas Clarke Luby.

Stephens may have acquired some useful knowledge from his contact with continental secret societies, but the system of organization he adopted was common to most secret societies. An oath was required, but there was some difficulty about the form because oath-bound societies were condemned by the church. Stephens's deputy, John O'Leary, thought the oath unnecessary and refused to take it.[47] There was some feeling that the oath should merely require obedience to superiors and that, once taken, secrecy would be imposed as a matter of course by local leaders. It does not appear that there was any uniform or consistent practice, but recruits were usually required to swear:

I, (A.B.), do solemnly swear, in the presence of God, to renounce all allegiance to the Queen of England; and do my utmost endeavour to make Ireland an independent, democratic republic; and that I shall take up arms and fight at a moment's warning, and shall yield implicit obedience to the commands of my superiors; and that I will observe inviolable secrecy with regard to the brotherhood, and finally I take this oath without mental reservations, so help me God.[48]

Stephens gave his organization the name of Irish Revolutionary Brotherhood (IRB), and took the title of Chief Organizer (COIRB). Each province of Ireland was to have a vice chief organizer who would swear in colonels. They in turn would swear in captains who would swear in sergeants. Sergeants were to recruit squads whom they were required to drill eight times a month. Subordinates would know only their immediate superiors and consequently could only betray a small section of the movement if caught by the authorities.[49]

Stephens insisted on absolute control over the organization. Only emissaries authorized by him could communicate with the American organization. Those who attempted to do so independently would be presumed traitors. O'Mahony was Stephens's deputy in America and in theory enjoyed similar power over the American organization. Such powers could be justified by the obvious need for secrecy, but they were equally useful to Stephens in convincing his American supporters that he was in command of a large movement. He offered to provide within three months 10,000 men, 1,500 with firearms and the rest armed with pikes. To accomplish this, he would need £80 to £100 a month. The Americans were also to send 500 trained men to Birmingham where they would purchase English rifles. Stephens must have realized that this was far beyond his resources, but felt that more modest figures would dampen American enthusiasm for the enterprise.[50]

Accompanied by Luby and Denieffe, Stephens made a second tour of Ireland, meeting in many cases the same people whom he had recently interviewed, but this time with a definite plan backed by the moral authority of his American supporters. A number of these local leaders agreed to act as officers in his organization and military studies were resumed along with nocturnal drilling on hillsides.

The existence of Stephens's organization was known almost immediately to the clergy and to Constitutionalist leaders such as A. M. Sullivan, the man who succeeded Gavan Duffy as editor of the *Nation*. Since the IRB represented a threat to their influence, and failure to take a firm stand would have the appearance of complicity, the clergy and liberal press soon denounced the new organization, which could hardly pass unnoticed by the authorities. As no precise information was offered, Stephens could not call his critics informers. Instead, he invented a new term — "Felon Setter" — by which he meant political criticism which provided information useful to the authorities.[51]

Young Irelanders who remained aloof from Stephens's organization and moderate journalists generally were sensitive to such charges, especially as they were often accompanied by threats and even physical assault from Fenian crowds. It is impossible to say how far the disclosure of information useful to the authorities was calculated, but the charge of "Felon Setter" proved an effective term of abuse. Apart from "Felon Setting", the Fenian movement faced the difficulty of genuine informers. This became evident when the Phoenix Society of Cork, an independent group which became associated with Stephens's organization, was denounced by an informer and its members arrested. As the informer, "Goulah" Sullivan, boasted openly of his deed, the handling of informers became a test of the ruthlessness of the organization. Yet Stephens and Luby rejected unconditionally all suggestions of reprisal.[52]

When Stephens returned from his second trip through Ireland, he was less concerned about Felon Setters and informers than he was about the mere £40 he had received from America. He at once concluded that it was necessary that he cross the Atlantic to secure the moral support of the Young Ireland exiles and, more particularly, to win over the New York Irish Republican Directory which had collected £5,000 for the aid of political prisoners.[53]

This proved an impossible task. Just as he had failed to win over the leading veterans of '48 such as John Blake Dillon, Stephens could hardly hope to succeed with their counterparts in America. He was received coolly by Doheny who told him that he could not hope to acquire Directory funds without the support of Dillon. When Stephens travelled to Knoxville, Tennessee, to visit Mitchel, he was accompanied as far as Washington, D. C., by Thomas Meagher and, incidentally, by D'Arcy McGee, who had business to conduct in the capital. In Washington, Stephens was introduced to President James Buchanan whom he described as a "Yankee Artful Dodger".[54]

McGee probably found common ground with Stephens who described America as the country "par excellence of upstart and ignorant brass".[55] While McGee, occupied with his Canadian venture, could hardly be a potential recruit, Stephens's quarrel at the moment was with his own followers, and he and McGee parted on friendly terms. On arriving in Knoxville, Stephens was received with courtesy by Mitchel who gave him fifty dollars, but would not support his campaign to raise money in the United States.[56] To these men of '48, with a secure place in revolutionary folklore, Stephens appeared to be an upstart with dubious credentials who wished to exploit their good names for the purpose of raising money. From Stephens's point of view, their refusal to lead a new movement imposed on them an obligation to place the prestige they had acquired at the disposal of those who, like himself, were prepared to continue the struggle.

A visit to Boston yielded only a trivial sum, yet before his departure from America, Stephens managed to collect £600.[57] He confirmed O'Mahony as his American deputy and secured the promise of further aid. It remained for O'Mahony to bring the various Irish republican clubs under his influence. With this in mind, O'Mahony drew upon his knowledge of Celtic folklore to select the name "Fenian" for the new organization, a name taken from "Fiana", the name of the ancient tribal militia[58] and of the present day regular army of Ireland.

Stephens and O'Mahony faced a formidable foe in Paul Cullen, the Archbishop of Dublin and Vicar Apostolic, whose influence extended across the Atlantic by means of the American church hierarchy. Cullen's antipathy to Fenianism was not shared by John MacHale, Archbishop of Tuam, who permitted clergy under his jurisdiction to maintain links with Fenians. In the American hierarchy, John Hughes, who became Archbishop of New York after 1850, supported Cullen's policy as did most of the hierarchy.[59] The Irish republicans blamed the church for the failure of previous rebellions and insisted that the political influence of the clergy was incompatible with the American system of government. It was not the church, however, but the Irish American press that presented the most immediate difficulties for the American Fenians.

O'Mahony's primary responsibility was to raise money for Stephens who had recommended the creation of a "Fair Trial Fund" to collect money for the defence of the Phoenix Society prisoners but which would be secretly diverted to conspiratorial purposes. This scheme was exposed in the *Irish American*[60] in what may have been a deliberate case of Felon Setting, and O'Mahony, who was in Ireland inspecting Stephens's forces, had to interrupt his visit to return to America. In his second responsibility, that of bringing the Irish military clubs under Fenian influence, O'Mahony was more successful and could soon take pride in a proliferation of Irish American military organizations such as the Irish Legion, the Irish Brigade, and O'Mahony's Guards.[61]

Stephens, who on leaving the United States made Paris his headquarters, was less successful. Like most revolutionaries, he was, and had to be, a gambler. In 1859 the brief tension between Britain and France, which gave rise to an invasion scare in England, induced Stephens to seek help from Louis Napoleon.[62] In the same year he attempted to bring into Ireland drill instructors from Britain, but was without funds to support those who came. A plan to hold a conference of Fenian colonels also failed for lack of funds.

By the time of the outbreak of the American Civil War, the Fenians had established a trans-Atlantic network extending as far as California, but they had yet to attract to themselves that blend of romantic nationalism and social indignation which had survived the rebellion of '98. They had asserted their claims but had not been accepted as the successors of the United Irishmen or the only legitimate heirs to the tradition of 1848.

### THE MAC MANUS FUNERAL

The Fenians were to acquire this heritage suddenly, almost by accident, as a result of the initiative of the California Fenians. Terrence Bellew MacManus, a veteran of '48 who had been exiled to Australia, escaped with Irish American aid and settled in San Francisco. He was not a Fenian and his death would have attracted little notice had not the Fenians turned his funeral into a trans-Atlantic political demonstration. Stephens at first was cool to this project but soon accepted it with enthusiasm.

The body of MacManus was to be returned to Ireland for burial, stopping at various centres with large Irish populations where suitable services would be held. The funeral procession across the country soon captured the imagination of the Irish Americans and it became difficult for the clergy, the Young Ireland exiles, or any section of the Irish community to ignore the proceedings. Archbishop Hughes paid tribute to the patriotism that had led MacManus to take up arms, even though unwisely.[63] In the face of the widespread popular support for the funeral, the one danger the Fenians faced was that the demonstration might be taken out of their hands and turned into a mere memorial service instead of a call to arms.

Moreover, the struggle between Fenians and moderates for control of the funeral service was complicated in Ireland by the plans of Doheny and others to make the funeral a signal for a general rising. Doheny's plan to seize the body from the Cork train which was carrying the funeral party was defeated by Stephens who kept the crowd at prayer while the train pulled out of the station bound for Dublin.[64]

On the eve of the funeral in Dublin Stephens triumphed a second time, in this case over the moderate nationalists such as Father Kenyon and others who tried to take the service out of his hands at the eleventh hour. Archbishop Cullen had forbidden clergy under his jurisdiction to participate in the service, but the prohibition was broken by Father Patrick Lavelle, a priest under the jurisdiction of Archbishop MacHale of Tuam. A procession seven miles long accompanied the body of MacManus through the streets of Dublin before a crowd estimated at 50,000, a demonstration which the jubilant Stephens regarded as a Fenian triumph over the influence of Constitutionalists and the hierarchy.[65]

Yet the MacManus funeral was essentially a peaceful demonstration. In pushing aside the Constitutionalists, the Fenians had adopted their methods. This might be a useful preliminary to the organization of an underground military movement, but the greater part of the financial and military resources of this trans-Atlantic conspiracy was in the United States. Given this imbalance, and the difficulties of using American resources in Ireland, American Fenians would inevitably look northward.

Although the idea of invading Canada would be resisted by both Stephens and O'Mahony, the only feasible objective for the kind of force that the American Fenians could raise was British America. The idea of "freeing Ireland on the plains of Canada", first raised in 1812 and again in 1848, would be raised once more if a crisis developed in Anglo-American relations.

# CHAPTER THREE

# Fenianism Takes Root in Canada

D'Arcy McGee arrived in Canada in May 1857, a year before the formal organization of the Fenian Brotherhood in New York and two years before the first Fenian circle was founded in Toronto. It was evident that McGee, who had already clashed with Irish republicans in New York, would have to wrestle with their Canadian auxiliaries. Yet the clash would not come until McGee had acquired influence in Canada and the Fenians had created an organization. It could not be a contest of equals as McGee, from the time of his arrival, had links with conventional politics to which the Canadian Fenians could never aspire. But McGee was an individual and against individuals organized groups, however small, could be formidable.

McGee came to Canada convinced that Irish immigrants could find in the British province an acceptance that had been denied them in the United States, and which they were unlikely to find under a system of secular republicanism. Although McGee's praise of Canada was generally congenial to Irish Canadians, there was dissent from his criticism of the United States. Irish nationalists in Canada, like their counterparts in the United States, preferred to contrast the poverty of the Irish at home with their success abroad, and did not think it useful to have this view marred by calling attention to Irish slums in American cities. Moreover, they were reluctant to quarrel with the Irish community in the United States, being inclined to regard the large numbers of Irish in the republic as evidence of their acceptance and influence.

Upon his arrival in Montreal, McGee started to publish the *New Era* in which he took up the familiar idea of a federation of the British American provinces and added a touch of poetry by writing of a "new nationality".[1] If McGee's O'Connellite style of politics was not easily adaptable to the American scene, he found the Canadian political atmosphere more congenial. Almost upon arrival, he accepted the invitation of the St. Patrick's Society to stand as the Irish Catholic candidate for Montreal in the general election of 1857.

McGee's idea of a new nationality was not particularly useful at that moment to any party or faction in Canadian politics, but it was closer to the ideas of the ruling conservative coalition of Cartier-Macdonald than to the various ideas of the opposition. The formidable editor of the Toronto *Globe,* George Brown, as leading figure in the divided opposition, advocated representation by population, or "rep. by pop.", which would have placed French Canada under an English majority, and he opposed giving public support to an independent Catholic school system. The only common ground shared by McGee and Brown was their opposition to the incorporation of the Orange Order. Yet both McGee and Brown had been journalists in the United States where they had acquired a distaste for republican institutions and both were attracted to more imaginative schemes of Canadian development in the West.

Running as an Irish Canadian candidate, McGee echoed the platform of Ogle Gowan in 1830 and that of Daniel Tracey in 1832, by asserting that, as one-third of the population of the constituency was Irish, one of the three candidates should be an Irishman.[2] Had one of the conservative candidates, among whom was George Cartier, been willing to stand down in favour of McGee, he might very well have entered Canadian politics as a conservative, but the best the conservatives were prepared to offer was a seat outside Montreal. Unwilling to gamble on separation from his Irish Catholic base in Montreal, McGee decided to run in company with Luther Holton, whose

views were much like those of Brown, and A. A. Dorion, a
nominal republican. All three opposition candidates were returned, leaving Cartier without a seat and with a dislike for
McGee whom he described as an adventurer.[3]

In running for office in the company of anti-clerical liberals,
McGee offended one of his original sponsors, George E. Clerk,
editor of the Montreal *True Witness,* a newspaper which enjoyed the patronage of Bishop Bourget of Montreal. Among
those who had invited him to run in the election was Bernard
Devlin, the prominent criminal lawyer who had spoken at the
Irish republican meeting in Montreal in 1848. It was unlikely
that Devlin would continue to support McGee if he quarrelled
publicly with the Irish republicans in the United States, and
Devlin, who was an ambitious man, would soon see McGee as
a political rival.

For the moment McGee included among his supporters that
section of the Irish Canadian community most likely to come
under Fenian influence. They were indispensable, in Montreal
at least, because McGee could not expect support from the
clergy. Moreover, if he was to find a place in Canadian politics,
it was necessary for him, as a liberal, to accept the Herculean
task of making George Brown acceptable to the Irish Catholic
electorate. This task in the long run proved impossible, yet it
provided McGee with an opportunity to show his political
talents and to gain a position of influence in Canadian politics.
At this time parliament met alternately in Quebec City and
Toronto. In the latter city he achieved his first success by becoming the hero of an accidental collision with Orangemen.

In an open letter to Canadians, McGee had denounced the
Orange Order as a secret society and was thus able to make the
most of his common ground with the opposition led by Brown.
The Orangemen were delighted to take up the challenge for
they found in McGee a former rebel and, as representative of
the Montreal Irish Catholic community, an ideal target.[4]

Partly as a reaction to attacks on July 12th parades, Orangemen had begun attacks on St. Patrick's Day processions. On
March 17, 1858, a Roman Catholic named Matthew Sheedy
was killed in Toronto, and the ground floor of the O'Donoghue National Hotel, where McGee was to address the St. Pat-

rick's Day gathering, was wrecked. McGee himself barely escaped with his life when a crowd of Orangemen noticed him returning to the hotel in a cab.[5] This incident gave McGee sufficient influence to persuade Toronto Irish Catholics to renounce St. Patrick's Day parades for three years, but he strained his popularity to the limit by refusing to insist that legislation be passed banning the July 12th Orange processions as well. What McGee wanted was voluntary renunciations on both sides.[6]

This riot, which happened to occur on the same day that Stephens founded the Irish Republican Brotherhood in Dublin,[7] was marked in Toronto by the establishment of the Hibernian Benevolent Society under the direction of Michael Murphy. Murphy was to become the leading figure among Canadian Fenians, but he does not appear to have been a Fenian at this time, and the society was dedicated simply to the defence of the Catholic community against Orangemen. It was at first nothing more than an assembly of the more aggressive elements of the Irish Catholics in Toronto prepared to carry on the historic feud with the Orangemen.[8]

Murphy was the type of man normally found at the head of Ribbon societies. He had once been a cooper by trade and was keeping a tavern on Esplanade Avenue. He had a flamboyant style of oratory which set limits to what he could accomplish in politics, but he had a gift for organizing demonstrations and arranging clandestine meetings. He was apparently attracted by the wider schemes of Fenianism and the challenge it offered to his talent. Murphy probably became a Fenian in 1859 when Edward O'Meagher Condon came to Toronto on a brief visit from New York and established the first Toronto Fenian Centre, but Murphy did not become Head Centre until 1860.[9] About sixty Fenians were recruited in the Toronto area,[10] undoubtedly enough to secure Murphy's control of the Hibernian Society, which numbered some six hundred.

During these early years, while McGee was making his way in Canadian politics, the Toronto Hibernians were not a conspicuous centre of dissent. McGee had been able to offset the hostility of the Lower Canadian clergy to George Brown by winning the confidence of Bishop Armand Charbonnel of

Toronto.[11] With Charbonnel's approval, McGee helped to secure Brown's return in the Toronto by-election of 1858 after the "Double Shuffle". Moreover, McGee organized a central committee, based on the St. Patrick's societies of five Upper Canadian counties. In organizing this committee, which was designed to deliver the Irish Catholic vote to approved candidates, McGee was aided by the Toronto journalist, James George Moylan, editor of the *Canadian Freeman*. McGee had given up his own paper, the *New Era*, by 1859 and was helping to sponsor Moylan's newspaper.[12] Had Charbonnel remained bishop for another decade, McGee's policy might have enjoyed greater success. But Charbonnel was succeeded in 1860 by John Joseph Lynch who preferred an alliance with the conservatives.[13] To understand Lynch's attitude towards McGee and the Fenians, it is necessary to glance at the attitude of the Irish hierarchy towards politics.

The head of the Irish church, Archbishop Paul Cullen, had had a long residence in Italy where he had been the principal link between the Vatican and the Irish church. His residence there had convinced him that secret societies were dangerous to the church. The case of Father Alessandro Gavazzi, a supporter of Garibaldi, who had subsequently toured the Western world denouncing the papacy, had made Cullen very suspicious of political priests. These attitudes were not shared by the Archbishop of Tuam, John MacHale, who had permitted a priest under his jurisdiction, Father Patrick Lavelle, to preside at the funeral of MacManus in Dublin, in defiance of Cullen.[14]

MacHale was an outspoken Irish nationalist. In forceful public statements, he placed responsibility for Irish poverty and the consequent exodus of the population on the British administration. MacHale was inclined to encourage all expressions of Irish nationalism, regretting, but at the same time forgiving, its more violent manifestations. Father Lavelle, who was in continuous contact with Fenians, wrote to the Canadian and American press seeking to collect money for Irish relief, and in these letters he lost no opportunity of denouncing the British administration in Ireland.[15]

Like MacHale, the new Catholic Bishop of Toronto, John Joseph Lynch, was given to denouncing British policy in Ireland and presenting the success of the Irish abroad as evidence of British responsibility for poverty in Ireland. On several occasions Lynch stated that he believed that the Irish had a mission to bring the English-speaking world back to the church and that for this mission it was necessary to preserve Irish nationality.[16] He was sympathetic to those who asserted their Irish nationality and, like MacHale, was inclined to ignore the existence of conspiratorial groups.

This was quite different from the view taken by Cullen and McGee who saw conspirators as exploiters, seeking popularity, influence, and in some cases money. For them, conspiracy was a demoralizing influence, damaging to the reputation of Irishmen, and a contributory cause of poverty.

Lynch, although praising the achievements of the Irish under Canadian institutions, did not contrast them favourably with conditions in the United States, and he was little concerned with the differences between a monarchy and a republic. In politics, Lynch sought to secure the best possible bargain for the Irish Catholic community without regard to party considerations. He had no sympathy with McGee's liberal alliance and was prepared to support the Orange Grand Master, John Hillyard Cameron, against Brown in the general election of 1861. Moylan at first followed McGee's policy, but withdrew his support for Brown in the course of the election, thus ensuring the victory of the Orange Grand Master.[17]

THE "TRENT" AFFAIR

The outbreak of the Civil War in the United States seemed to underline McGee's warning about the instability of American institutions and brought on a crisis in Anglo-American relations at the end of 1861. The occasion for this was the seizure of two Confederate agents who were travelling on the British steamer, the *Trent*. This act was widely applauded in the American press in which British protests were greeted by threats to invade Canada. The New York *Herald* declared that two-thirds of the Canadian population favoured annexation to the United States.[18]

McGee understood that Irish republicans in the United
States would give assurance that the Irish in Canada would
support invasion, and he was concerned lest this be taken
seriously by other Canadians. In an effort to make his own
sentiments clear, he refused an invitation to address the New
England Society of Montreal which he had previously accepted.[19] At the same time, he took an active part in efforts to
raise militia volunteers. Public meetings of French Canadians
and Scots were passing unanimous resolutions calling for the
raising of distinctive national units, and it was assumed that
the Irish would do the same. This would appeal to the martial
spirit of Irish Canadians, but they also took pride in the
presence of Corcoran's Irish Brigade serving in the Northern
Armies. In Toronto, efforts to raise Irish units were treated
with coolness by militia authorities, but in Montreal the
mixed loyalties of the Irish found expression in opposition to
recruiting.[20] This was the result of what was probably the
unplanned collusion between McGee's local enemies and a
dozen or so Fenians who came up from Vermont[21] to disrupt
the meeting in Montreal called to raise Irish volunteers.

McGee, whose brother was serving in Corcoran's Brigade,
declared his sympathy with the Northern cause, but also
insisted on the need of the Canadian Irish to resist the
threatened invasion. When he spoke of raising troops there
were shouts of "not under the British flag", and throughout
the meeting, he was interrupted by cheers for the United
States and for Corcoran's Brigade. Yet McGee persisted. "There
is no land, since the Irish race had a place in history, where
the Irish name and honor are so much respected as in Canada," he declared. "The man who will not defend the country
does not deserve to be harbored for a single night in it."
Cheers and groans greeted McGee's statements and proved
sufficient to disrupt the meeting, and at one point McGee
threatened to dictate his speech to the press. In spite of this,
and in the face of evidence to the contrary, the meeting ended
with the desired resolutions declaring unanimous support for
the raising of an Irish battalion.[22]

Among the hostile demonstrators, McGee recognized Owen
J. Devlin, brother of Bernard Devlin, and members of the

Prince of Wales's regiment of militia which Bernard Devlin later commanded. In a letter to the Montreal *Herald* signed "Civis Canadiensis", McGee expressed his fear and condemnation of the Fenian presence in Canada.[23] But the *Trent* affair was soon settled and McGee was not anxious to attract further attention to disloyalty among Irish Canadians.

Meanwhile, in Dublin, the Irish Constitutionalist, A. M. Sullivan, Gavan Duffy's successor as editor of the *Nation,* and The O'Donoghue, MP, a nephew of Daniel O'Connell and Chieftain of the Glens, thought to use the excitement aroused by the *Trent* affair to launch a new national organization. The theme was to be that England's difficulties were Ireland's opportunity, and that Irish resources should be withheld from the war effort as a means of forcing concessions from the British government.

Stephens saw this as an effort to take from the Fenians the political initiative which he had seized during the MacManus funeral. To maintain his ascendancy, Stephens sought to make the Fenian presence felt in such a way that the Constitutionalists understood that they spoke by leave of the Fenians. Resolutions could be passed only with Fenian consent and, by organized shouting and selective applause, the Fenians attempted to create the impression that there was an impatience with moderate measures and a rising disposition to use physical force. Above all, Stephens was determined to prevent the creation of a new constitutionalist organization.[24]

Stephens reported his success to O'Mahony early in 1862, writing that, "We are so thoroughly master of this city [Dublin], that in the event of a public meeting of the enemy, we can take them over and flog them through the streets. . . . If John Mitchel, William Smith O'Brien, The O'Donoghue, and all that . . . were to meet here tomorrow against our wish, we could do anything with them we like."[25]

Few Fenians in North America were aware of Stephens's antipathy towards the Constitutionalists, for all nationalist meetings were reported in the Irish American press as evidence of discontent in Ireland. Apart from this, the American Fenians were throwing their energies into the Northern war effort. O'Mahony reported that enlistments in the Northern forces had dissolved fifty Fenian centres[26] and he himself served for four months as commander of O'Mahony's Guards, keeping watch over Confederate prisoners of war.

Yet Stephens could not reconcile the apparent strength of the American Fenians with the "one hundred and thirteen pounds from the whole American movement in one year". In February 1863 he sent his agent, Thomas Clarke Luby, on a tour of the Northern states,[27] but when Luby returned in November with a mere £100, Stephens realized that he could expect nothing from America in the immediate future.[28] Although he claimed to have a large underground force at his command, Stephens appears to have virtually suspended activities in 1863, finding time to marry and take up gardening.

TORONTO FENIANS

In Toronto, Michael Murphy, left without guidance from Fenians in Ireland or the United States, built up the Hibernian Society as a Canadian organization dedicated to the cause of Irish nationalism and sought to establish a network of branches throughout the province. As long as Fenianism was dormant in Ireland and America, Murphy's Hibernian Society was in practice an Irish Canadian club concerned with Irish affairs and accepting the Canadian system of government in its existing form.

It is not surprising, then, that Murphy was able to secure Bishop Lynch's approval for the resumption of the St. Patrick's Day parades which had been suspended in Toronto since 1858.[29] When this first procession in three years ended peacefully with three cheers for the Pope, the Queen, and the Bishop, Murphy enjoyed a minor triumph, having established not only the importance of the Hibernian Society but its respectability. Even Moylan's *Canadian Freeman* congratulated him for his restoration of Irish prestige in Toronto.[30]

Moylan was less happy about the founding of the *Irish Canadian* under Hibernian patronage at the opening of 1863, if only because it added to the number of Irish journals in Toronto.[31] Its editor, Patrick Boyle, was not a Fenian and he had from time to time secured Catholic votes for John A. Macdonald's party. Boyle undoubtedly was aware of Murphy's Fenian associations but saw no danger in the connection. One of the purposes of the *Irish Canadian* was to reprint selected articles from the Irish and the Irish American press which, whatever the tone of their politics, might be offered as evidence that Irish nationalism was alive. D'Arcy McGee had never favoured this practice because republican and revolutionary sentiments expressed outside of Canada might raise doubts about the loyalty of Irish Canadians.

Yet the *Irish Canadian* did not hesitate to rebuke the *Irish American* when it described Canada as a "paradise for fools" and disputed the Boston *Pilot*'s contention that "the human race decreases and degenerates in Canada".[32] To counter charges that he was circulating republican propaganda, Boyle printed strongly worded royalist editorials in the *Irish Canadian*.[33] These were consistent with the O'Connellite principles which Boyle presumably retained and probably did not trouble Murphy's Fenian conscience. Like most of the Fenian rank and file, Murphy had little interest in the republic as a form of government.

The first few issues of the *Irish Canadian* could hardly be distinguished from those of the *Canadian Freeman* with regard to policy. Both papers published Archbishop MacHale's letter which offered outspoken condemnation of British rule in Ireland, and both printed Father Lavelle's appeals for Irish relief which were invariably exercises in nationalist propaganda. At this time Lavelle was vice-president of the Brotherhood of St. Patrick, an organization that would be condemned by Archbishop Cullen before the end of the year. In the United States, O'Mahony's Fenians were the principal agents of Lavelle's charities. In one of his widely circulated appeals, Lavelle wrote, "The youth of this country [Ireland] feel they are slaves, and there is a spirit within them that no power, no influence, no condemnation will be able to subdue until it triumphs."[34] Yet Lavelle was working in Ireland independently of Stephens who protested that Lavelle's charities were diverting funds from the "sinews of war".[35] Lavelle's charities, although a useful means of propaganda, were not, like the Fair

Trial Fund of 1858, a collection agency for the Fenians.

Murphy enjoyed a second triumph in 1863 when Bishop Lynch agreed to address the Hibernians and the other societies participating in the St. Patrick's Day parade. Lynch declared that this and the many other celebrations held that day were evidence that the spirit of Irish nationality was alive among the Irish overseas. Speaking immediately after the Bishop, Murphy referred to a great movement for the liberation of Ireland gathering on both sides of the Atlantic and he spoke of The O'Donoghue in such a way as to suggest that the Irish Constitutionalists and the Irish American republicans were somehow moving towards a united effort for the liberation of Ireland. There was no public reference to Fenianism as its leaders were not yet prepared to admit its existence.[36]

The Orange *Leader* was offended by Murphy's "treasonable utterances"[37] and the *Globe* made belligerent references to Hibernian disloyalty.[38] Boyle wrote a conciliatory comment on the *Leader*'s hostility and directed his attack against the *Globe*. He found the Scots responsible for the rising of 1837 on the grounds that William Lyon Mackenzie was a Scot. "There was a quiet calculating republican vein that runs through the blood" of the Scots, Boyle wrote, and consequently through the blood of George Brown of the *Globe*. To Boyle, the Irish were a body of men "monarchical in all their tendencies".[39] Boyle gave the Irish the credit for putting down the rebellion of 1837, repudiating by implication the Irish associates of the Patriots, Drs. E. A. Theller and E. B. O'Callaghan.

A week later, Boyle praised Louis Napoleon for declaring Algeria an Arab monarchy and himself King, setting an example, Boyle declared, that Queen Victoria might follow in Ireland.[40] In the same issue he announced his pleasure at the forthcoming marriage of the Prince of Wales, while Father Lavelle's declaration that the celebrations in Ireland of the Prince's engagement "fill us with shame" must have caused some embarrassment.[41]

D'Arcy McGee took no public notice of the Hibernians in Toronto at this time, but he was aware of efforts to form a branch of the society in Montreal and took time to warn of the dangers of secret societies. McGee received a mild rebuke for this in the *Irish Canadian*[42] which was perhaps intended as a warning. Nevertheless, when McGee was dropped from the John Sandfield Macdonald cabinet and decided to run as an independent, the *Irish Canadian* expressed qualified sympathies for McGee with whom they apparently had no wish to quarrel. Nor did they regret the bitter exchange between Macdonald and McGee. When Macdonald taunted McGee with being an alien who "had no right to dictate to native born Canadians", McGee retorted, "The man who taunts me with being an alien . . . spits upon the grave of his own grandfather."[43]

Meanwhile, the New York *Tablet,* formerly McGee's *American Celt,* attacked both O'Mahony and Father Lavelle, ridiculing the idea of an American secret society liberating Ireland. Lavelle's reply was quoted in the *Irish Canadian* on June 17. He argued that any society that aimed at liberating Ireland was of necessity secret.[44]

To these difficulties of reconciling loyalty in Canada with rebellion in Ireland was added a new embarrassment for Irish Canadians, brought on by the anti-draft riots in New York and Philadelphia. Although the Irish in America had supplied more than their share of volunteers for the Federal forces, they took the lead in resisting the draft which would fall more heavily on them than on other sections of the community, if only because few Irishmen could afford to buy exemption from military service by hiring substitutes.

The *Globe,* as the leading supporter of the Northern cause in Canada, was delighted to present the riots as evidence of the chronic discontent of the Irish.[45] In reply, Boyle virtually ignored the riots, denying, without much conviction, that they were of Irish origin.[46] By this time, Fenian efforts to keep Irish military units up to strength made the Fenians in effect recruiting agents for the United States forces on both sides of the Atlantic. Moreover, the Fenian argument that service in the Federal forces would provide useful training for the eventual liberation of Ireland could be employed by all recruiting agents.

In August, the *Irish Canadian* noted that Irish independence "depended on a Northern victory as England must become the object of United States aggression in the event of a Federal victory." The editor commented, "America has become a great military power, but Ireland would rally to England's defence if the Act of Union was repealed."[47]

With the obvious growth of unrest in Ireland and reports of secret society activity in America, Archbishop Cullen called a meeting of Irish bishops in September 1863 when he restated the church's attitude towards secret societies. He banned the Brotherhood of St. Patrick, a group of little importance but easier to identify than the Fenians.[48] There were similar condemnations by American bishops and a pastoral by Bishop Ignace Bourget of Montreal in which he condemned secret societies.[49] The latter pastoral was read in Montreal with considerable force by Father Patrick Dowd of St. Patrick's Church. Yet McGee later claimed that Fenian sympathizers were able to neutralize the effect of the pastoral by insisting, as they left the church, that the condemnation was a formality which had to be observed but not taken seriously.[50]

Boyle met these attacks on secret societies with new assertions of loyalty, declaring that "monarchy is best suited for the soil of Ireland . . . had Ireland only the liberty enjoyed in Canada".[51] Yet this declared preference for monarchy in Ireland as well as in Canada was combined with praise for the contemporary uprising in Poland, in which the Irish hierarchy's insistence upon constitutionalism was contrasted with the Polish clergy's support of armed resistance. The Irish bishops were referred to as ornaments of the church, and the *Irish Canadian* asked how "can the Bishops quell the demands of human nature?"[52] Boyle delighted in reporting the strong language used at Constitutionalist meetings in Ireland, and in editorial comment attempted to give the impression that the Irish, finally driven beyond endurance, would follow the example of the Poles.

These references in the *Irish Canadian* to Irish unrest provoked an editorial in the *Globe*[53] under the heading "Disloyal Hibernians" and this in turn, because of its anti-Irish tone, brought a rebuke from the Orange *Leader*.[54] Boyle seemed grateful for the latter and took the occasion to renew his attacks on the Scots for their disloyalty in 1837. In the midst

of this dispute, reports began to arrive of the convention of
the American Fenians in Chicago during the first week of
November 1863.[55]

## REVIVAL OF AMERICAN FENIANISM

As the American organization began to recover from the im-
pact of the Civil War, O'Mahony was faced with a revolt of the
Midwestern Fenians who demanded that he call a convention
of American Fenians.[56] This move was essentially an attack on
his personal leadership, but it also represented a growing demand for the Americanization of the movement. Such Americanization would hardly have increased the flow of funds to
Stephens, but there was a danger that the opponents of
O'Mahony might use the prestige of Stephens to depose
O'Mahony. Under the existing system, Stephens was Head
Centre of the Fenian Brotherhood, and O'Mahony acted as
his American deputy. In order to defeat the Midwestern opposition and secure himself against any further intrusion of
Stephen's authority, O'Mahony accepted the demand for a
convention and used it to reconstitute what was, in theory,
the American wing of a united organization into an independent American voluntary association with himself as chief.

In spite of the disputes which had induced O'Mahony to
call the convention, he was able to dominate the proceedings
and to maintain the appearance of harmony. The convention
opened on November 3, 1863, attended by eighty-two delegates
who represented twelve states, the armies of the Potomac,
Cumberland, and Tennessee, and Washington, D.C.[57] Michael
Murphy was probably present as a representative of Toronto,
accompanied by delegates from Montreal, Quebec City, and
Hamilton.[58]

Under the new system, the Head Centre was to be elected
annually at a general convention of representatives of state
centres in which each circle of one hundred members could
send one delegate, and those with over two hundred members
were eligible to send two delegates. The Head Centre would
nominate a council with the approval of the convention and

the council would then elect its own officers, including the
president of the council. Financial matters were to be controlled by the convention.

Some aspects of the old system were retained, as State Centres
were appointed by the Head Centre upon the recommendation
of a majority of local circles and could be removed by the Head
Centre with the consent of the council. O'Mahony resigned as
Head Centre but was unanimously re-elected and his recom-
mendations for council were approved. As Stephens's deputy,
O'Mahony had in theory no right to undertake such far-reach-
ing measures without consulting the Irish Head Centre, but,
as Stephens had no organized party at the convention, the
revolutionary aspects of O'Mahony's action could be ignored.[59]

The convention adopted twenty-one resolutions of which
three were supposedly secret. One was a pledge to establish
the Irish republic; the other two acknowledged Stephens as
Head of the European movement, a respected ally but in no
way senior to the American Head Centre.[60] This was further
emphasized by a published declaration that interference on the
part of those receiving instructions from foreign potentates or
officials—which could apply to both the Pope and to Stephens
—was repudiated.[61]

In his policy statement, O'Mahony declared, "Being an
American association and basing our rights of action upon our
privileges as American citizens, we can place Ultra Montagne
plotters in an awkward position and a very unsafe one for them
if they presume to assail us. The pretext "Secret" Society
being taken away from them, they will be forced to assail us
as a political organization. They must avow that the Papacy
has made common cause with the tyrants of Europe to put
down republican propaganda."[62]

O'Mahony argued that the Irish hierarchy, acting in the
British interest, was influencing the American Catholic hierarchy to take measures against Fenianism and that this constituted intervention in American politics: "Were we to submit
to their dictation in such matters, Know Nothingness would
become a patriotic duty and our American-born fellow citizens
might justly declare us unworthy of co-partnership in national
sovereignty. We would be mere subjects of England through

the political adherents [the American hierarchy] of Dr.
Cullen."[63] Young Fenians not already in the armed forces
were urged to study military tactics and to organize companies
to support the United States in any future war with Great
Britain.[64] War with Britain was the duty of the American
government and Fenians were prepared to proceed to British
territory by the shortest route, presumably the Canadian
frontier.[65]

Yet there was no declaration of support for the federal war
effort. Most Fenians were War Democrats, but the organization
included a number of Copperheads, or Confederate sympathizers. A Fenian oath was published in which there was no
reference to secrecy, but the Fenians were bound to obey the
orders of their officers, and it was privately understood that
they could enforce secrecy.[66]

The Fenian challenge to the hierarchy provoked no general
condemnation of Fenianism by the church. Priests under the
jurisdiction of the bishops of Chicago and Philadelphia were
instructed to deny the sacraments to Fenians and Fenian
sympathizers. In New York the Catholic *Freeman's Journal*
found nothing objectionable about the Fenians, but changed
its attitude after the action of the Bishop of Chicago. Replies
to an enquiry on the question of Fenianism, sent out by the
Archbishop of Baltimore, indicated a reluctance among American bishops to take a stand on the Fenians. As a result, it was
decided to adopt no general policy and the majority of bishops
decided to leave the Fenians undisturbed for the time being.[67]

LOYALTY AND THE TORONTO HIBERNIANS

In Toronto, Hibernian assurances of loyalty were less creditable
after the Chicago convention as it became impossible to ignore
the existence of the American Fenians. With the American
Fenians openly committed to the use of force and condemned
as a secret society by leading bishops in the United States, it
was more difficult to speak as though the Constitutionalists
in Ireland and the Irish republicans in the United States were
part of a great spontaneous movement. Boyle began by insist-

ing that the published rules of the Fenian Brotherhood proved that it was not a secret society and that a purely American society could not be subversive to Canadian institutions.[68]

A similar view of Fenianism was offered in Ireland by John Martin whose efforts to revive the "Repeal" movement had been reported in the *Irish Canadian*. Like Boyle, Martin insisted that the Fenians were a public organization and purely American. He could understand the bitterness of Irish Americans against England, but he insisted that this was not shared by the Irish at home. An American-based invasion of Ireland, he added, presupposed an Anglo-American war and, in such an event, the Americans would invade Canada and the West Indies before they would consider Ireland.[69]

At the same time that this material appeared in the *Irish Canadian*, the *Canadian Freeman* commented that the Irish in the United States were striving to "convince the world that praise of American institutions is deserved" and when criticism of American institutions was offered, the Irish "were not only sensitive but unreasonable".[70] Yet Boyle made no attempt to contradict the arguments of Martin or to praise American institutions himself. He merely insisted that the Fenians, because of their numbers and military training, were formidable and that, since they hoped to liberate Ireland, they deserved sympathy.

Yet the increasing references to the growing impatience of the Irish people with petitions and speeches in parliament, when added to the clerical condemnation of Fenians, would have presented the Toronto Hibernians with a serious difficulty had it not been for Archbishop MacHale. By publicly thanking Father Lavelle for his Fenian-sponsored charities early in 1864, MacHale provided the movement with a claim to clerical approval.[71] Moreover, when O'Mahony's opponents among the American Fenians decided to hold a fair in Chicago and invited Stephens to attend, MacHale sent three autographed portraits of himself to be sold at what was a thinly disguised effort to acquire the "sinews of war".[72]

This event, advertised in the *Irish Canadian* as the "Fenian Fair", received editorial support from Boyle who declared that the Fenians were the "greatest organization for amelioration of

Irish grievances since the days of the United Irishmen".[73]
Although the amount raised was trivial, support of the Fenian
Fair in theory, at least, constituted support of the projected
invasion of Ireland. Apart from a token financial support
openly given to American Fenians, the Hibernians in Toronto
were acquiring arms and undertaking military training,
ostensibly for defence against Orangemen—measures consistent
with the instructions that O'Mahony had given to Fenians to
acquire military training for the ultimate purpose of liberating Ireland.

Conspiracy for a distant purpose, involving no immediate
risks, and carried out amid the indignant protests of the *Globe*
and the *Leader,* would give the Toronto Fenians a sense of
participating in great events so essential to the morale of the
organization. Yet their continued influence within the Catholic
community was dependent on reconciling their support of
Fenianism with Canadian loyalism.

In seeking to accomplish this, Boyle had to mix a larger
amount of falsehood with the ambiguities and misleading statements that had hitherto been sufficient. In reply to one of
George Brown's frequent attacks on the Hibernians, Boyle replied that he did not believe that the purpose of the Fenians
was to dissolve the connection between Ireland and the Crown.
Brown, he repeated, belonged to that "rebly class who sought
to wrest this colony from the British Crown."[74] Boyle, and even
Murphy, might have been happier had the Fenians been less
candid about their republicanism, but in the United States
the Irish could not afford to neglect their one substantial bond
of sympathy with the majority of Americans.

As long as the Toronto Hibernians retained the confidence
of Bishop Lynch, it was unnecessary for them to convince the
*Globe* and the *Leader* of their loyalism. They still retained
his confidence by March 17, 1864, for Lynch appeared with
Murphy to address the crowd after the annual parade. On this
occasion, Lynch again spoke of the evils arising out of the
poverty in Ireland and the anomaly of a heavily endowed Protestant church in a Catholic country. Speaking immediately
after the bishop, Murphy repeated the charges of the Scots'
disloyalty in 1837.[75] Yet, when referring to Ireland, he asked

what was to be done when constitutional protests were re-
peatedly ignored. The clergy, he declared, were opposed to
bloodshed but would be with the people "when the time for
bloodshed came".[76]

Statements like this would provoke nothing more than the
passing indignation of the *Globe* and *Leader,* but the Toronto
Hibernians were at this point embarrassed by the more articulate expressions of the Hibernians in Montreal. This smaller
and less cautious group, which included many personal enemies of McGee, held a dinner on St. Patrick's Day in competition with the official dinner of the St. Patrick's Society. In contrast to two thousand at the official celebration, about one
hundred attended the Hibernian dinner, but they enlivened
the festivities with rebel toasts and Fenian songs, all of which
was reported to McGee. He at once denounced the dinner as a
Fenian affair, regretting that even one hundred could be attracted to it and hinted vaguely at the Fenian presence in
Toronto.[77]

A few weeks earlier, the *Irish Canadian* had complimented
McGee for sustaining his reputation for oratory when speaking
on immigration.[78] Although the Toronto Hibernians did not
support McGee's policy, they had no desire to start a feud with
him, but were compelled to do so after the attack on their
Montreal brethren. McGee was denounced as the "Goulah of
Griffintown", a reference to the informer, "Goulah" Sullivan,
who had betrayed the Phoenix Society of Cork in 1858.[79] This
outburst against McGee led the *Canadian Freeman* to refer to
the *Irish Canadian* as the "Fenian organ", bringing to the sur-
face a latent antagonism between the two journals which had
been smouldering since 1863.[80] Boyle was then forced to com-
mence a feud with Moylan which lasted for the balance of the
year.

The Hibernians passed a series of resolutions denying all
connection with the Fenian Brotherhood which they said "was
established for a different purpose".[81] This was literally true,
and might have been sufficient to quiet the fears of sympathizers who were anxious to help if they were not risking association with avowed revolutionaries. Yet it would not satisfy

those who were either hostile to Fenianism or determined to avoid Fenian connections.

The Hibernians faced a growing isolation within their own community which became more explicit when Bishop Farrell of Hamilton denounced the local Hibernians as a secret society.[82] Moreover, the respectable cover provided by MacHale and Lavelle was wearing thin as Archbishop Cullen's quarrel with Lavelle became public. Moylan, a former friend of Lavelle, supported Archbishop Cullen and made unflattering comments about the enthusiasms of Archbishop MacHale.[83]

In efforts to reassert their Catholic orthodoxy and to reconcile it with their support of physical force in Ireland, the Hibernians looked for precedents in the defence of the Papal States by Pius IX and to the current insurrection in Poland.[84] Ignoring the absence of a constitutional alternative to rebellion in Poland and the increasing evidence that the rebellion had failed, they insisted that, as Ireland's grievances were equal to those of Poland, they should find a similar remedy. This argument was reinforced by praise of Pope Pius IX as the only sovereign in Europe to support the Poles.[85]

In spite of such support for physical force, Boyle still expressed sympathy for the efforts of the Constitutionalists in Ireland. He publicly regretted the disruption of a meeting in Dublin held to protest the raising of a statue to Prince Albert in that city, not realizing that the disruptions were the work of Irish Fenians. Moreover, the Hibernians still enjoyed the confidence of Bishop Lynch, who aroused their enthusiasm by a speech in which he argued that the prevalence of crime among the Irish in Toronto, as revealed in recent statistics, was the result of the loosening of family ties caused by immigration. "Among the dangers to which the lapse of parental authority exposes the young," he insisted, "was the temptation to join secret societies like the Fenians."[86] Yet, as Lynch censured British rule in Ireland as the cause of emigration, even the Irish Fenians were prepared to forgive his condemnation of Fenianism, and Lynch's speech was printed in the Fenian-controlled *Irish People* in Dublin.[87]

Boyle also felt bound to praise as a great day for Ireland the

celebration of the centennial of Daniel O'Connell's birth, celebrations that marked the opening of a new Constitutionalist
campaign which was supported by Archbishop Cullen.[88] The
inconsistency of supporting constitutionalism and insurrection
at the same time undoubtedly embarrassed Boyle, yet it reflected the attitude of his readers who disliked hearing any
manifestation of Irish nationalism criticized.

FENIAN FEVER

The Hibernians were rescued temporarily from their growing
inconsistencies by the reaction in Belfast to an O'Connell
memorial meeting in Dublin. To the Orangemen, this appeared as a demonstration of the power and unity of the Catholic community and the beginning of a new and powerful Constitutional movement. Belfast experienced several days of
rioting during which Daniel O'Connell was burned in effigy
and some eight people were seriously injured.[89]

It seems likely that Murphy at first expected similar riots in
Toronto and he began preparing his organization for them.
The Hibernians had obviously undertaken some military training during the six years of their existence, which probably improved their marching on St. Patrick's Day. On receiving news
of the Belfast riots, Murphy evidently sought to bring his
organization to perfection by secret drilling and collecting
weapons. He was arrested in Buffalo after efforts to purchase
revolvers, but was released when Sergeant Major Cummins of
the Toronto police, not realizing Murphy's purpose, gave assurances as to his character. Pikes were made and a variety of
weapons collected in anticipation of a coming conflict.[90]

As the Orangemen had held their July 12th parade in
Hamilton instead of Toronto,[91] the Hibernians had to build
up their case for an Orange threat on the basis of Orange history and the recent riots in Belfast. Yet this was sufficient to
lend an element of probability to rumours, possibly spread by
Murphy, that the Toronto Orangemen planned to burn Daniel
O'Connell, the Pope, and the Duke of Newcastle in effigy on

Guy Fawkes Day, November 5, which was also the birthday of King William of Orange.[92]

Indoor celebrations were held on the evening of November 5, but Orangemen marched about after the dinner, playing Protestant tunes on the fife and drums before returning home. It is possible that the Hibernians expected to interrupt the anticipated burnings in effigy, but they made no move until after the Orangemen had gone home. Then, close to midnight, about four hundred armed, masked Hibernians gathered near Queen's Park, keeping a nucleus there and sending columns to the east and west of the city. About two hours later, they fired shots in different parts of the city, presumably a signal to disperse.[93] The timing suggests that Murphy had no intention of provoking a clash with the Orangemen, but rather that the mobilization was an exercise to raise Hibernian morale and perhaps to impress Torontonians with their strength. If this was the case, they were highly successful. The demonstration created a minor Fenian "bogey" which anticipated the more general reaction of the country in 1866.

In describing the foray of the Hibernians, the *Leader*[94] was more restrained than the *Globe,* noting from police reports that the Hibernian demonstrators were labourers, shoemakers, tavern-keepers, and shop assistants.[95] The *Globe* protested against an "armed organization existing in disregard of the law", and suggested that the mayor should call out the military.[96] Both newspapers reported rumours that arms were kept in the offices of Catholic newspapers and in churches.[97] A tavern-keeper named John MacGuire was arrested when pikes were discovered on the premises of his establishment, while Sergeant Major Cummins was suspended from the police force when it was discovered that he had secured Michael Murphy's release in Buffalo where the Hibernian chief had been detained in connection with his purchase of arms.[98]

Bishop Lynch addressed a letter to the press deploring the midnight demonstration but declared that the church had no power to deny Catholics the right of self-defence against the Orangemen.[99] Both the *Globe* and *Leader*[100] found the Bishop's letter unsatisfactory, insisting that there was no evidence of an immediate Orange threat to Catholics and that the rumoured threat of the burning of O'Connell in effigy was not a justification for an armed demonstration.

As there was no evidence that pikes were used in the demonstration, MacGuire was released from custody.[101] Similarly, Sergeant Major Cummins was restored to duty on the police force as it was obvious that Cummins had had no reason to believe that Murphy had been purchasing arms for illegal purposes. Yet the mayor, F. H. Medcalf, was not satisfied. He resigned as chairman of the Police Board in protest against Cummins's reinstatement, but had to withdraw his resignation when he learned that, as mayor, he was obliged by law to remain chairman of the Police Board.[102]

The general impression left on readers of the *Leader* and the *Globe* was one of official incompetence in the face of a serious threat abetted by clerical connivance. The *Globe* declared that it was not a question of a dispute between Orangemen and Fenians, but of law and order.[103]

The editors of the *Irish Canadian* had no reason to be surprised at the reaction, but began to show signs of alarm at its intensity. Since the Hibernians could neither deny their connection with the demonstration nor offer evidence of an immediate provocation, they again tried to make the most of the Belfast riots[104] and the history of Orangeism. With this material they could make a plausible case, but they faced the disadvantage of having united against themselves the formidable combination of the Orangemen and George Brown.

The *Irish Canadian* asserted that half the militia of Toronto were Orangemen[105] and insisted that the Catholics could expect no protection from the mayor who was also an Orangeman. To strengthen their case, they cited previous Orange riots in Toronto and, in an effort to associate attacks on Catholics with Americanism, they referred to the Philadelphia riots of 1847 and the burning of Catholic homes in Louisville, Kentucky, by Know-Nothing elements in 1855. They then repeated the familiar charges of Grit disloyalty, warning that, "When the Hibernians, like the Grits, look to Washington for relief, they may be charged with designed subvertiveness to British rule. They are neither Fenians, rebels, or members of a secret society."[106]

The *Globe* continued to print letters that reflected the growing panic in areas where denominational tensions existed. Early in December, Father Northgraves of Barrie complained in letters to the press that rumours were circulating that he was drilling Fenians in his church, yet at the same time he insisted that Fenianism was a consequence of Orangeism.[107] John Hillyard Cameron protested that the "highest quarters of the Church of Rome" were justifying Fenianism on the grounds of an Orange threat,[108] but he cautioned Orangemen not to disturb the peace.[109] In letters to the press, Murphy again denied that the Hibernians were Fenians, but approved the purpose of Fenians and "all others seeking the liberation of Ireland".[110]

The rising tide of panic and controversy reached a climax in the middle of December when rumours that Fenian bands had burned a Presbyterian church and Orange hall[111] caused farmers to arm themselves and to gather in crowds. The areas affected were on the line between York and Vaughan in Adjala, Tecumseh, and Peel. Undoubtedly, fears in these areas were blended with ready acceptance of a quarrel in which the Protestants might claim just provocation and were clearly the stronger party. Nine companies of volunteers in the Toronto area offered their services to the government, obviously pleased with the prospect of active service.[112]

Even the governor, Lord Monck, began to be alarmed. To Sir Fenwick Williams, the commander of the British forces in Canada, Monck confessed, "The 'Fenian' movement in Toronto gives me some uneasiness, especially with respect to the security of the arms of the Volunteers" which were stored in a wooden drill shed. He suggested the propriety of placing a sentry in a position to command the drill hall in order to "guard against a simple theft of the arms at night", but to do it without attracting public attention "to our movements or dignify these vagabonds into the position of public enemies".[113]

Realizing the danger, the *Globe* sought to quiet public opinion and published no more alarmist letters to the editor, and the panic subsided. Yet rumours of this excitement reached as far as Halifax where Reverend D. F. Hutchinson, Orange Grand Chaplain of Nova Scotia and editor of the *Burning Bush*, wrote of "12,000 Fenians organized and ready to rise".[114] The Archbishop of Nova Scotia, T. L. Connolly, felt it necessary to ridicule the idea that Catholic churches were used as arsenals and to emphasize the church's opposition to Fenianism.[115] In Montreal, the *Herald* declared that the Hibernians had as much right to self-defence as the Orangemen,[116] while the *True Witness* found that, save for the assertions of the editor of the *Globe*,[117] there was no evidence that Hibernians were Fenians.

In this instance, Catholic leaders had publicly accepted the Hibernian contention that their demonstration was a response to the existence of Orangeism and they refused to treat the Hibernians as a Fenian agency. It was the more cautious policy to take since it would be impossible to join in the clamour against the Fenians without adding to the general alarm and it provided time to deal with the Fenians as an internal problem of the Catholic community.

The Hibernian contention that they were merely a response to the threat of Orangeism would have been creditable had Murphy been less outspoken about Ireland's grievances. At the end of the year, the *Leader* observed, under the heading "Treasonable Writing", that Murphy had recommended rebellion as a cure for Ireland's grievances. The *Leader* urged that the Catholic community "should silence Murphy . . . if such means are not taken, worse will happen . . . . The Bishop should do his duty."[118]

D'Arcy McGee, like other leading Catholics, did not think public attacks on Fenians expedient at this time. In an address to the St. Patrick's Society in Montreal, he dismissed Brown's claim that there were 1,500 Fenians in Montreal. Although aware of the existence of a sizable movement in the city, McGee insisted that there could not be more than fifteen without his hearing of it.[119] Secret service reports indicated that there were probably about 350 organized Fenians in Montreal at the end of 1865, and McGee was aware that one hundred had attended the Hibernian dinner on March 17, 1864.[120]

McGee's private thoughts on Fenians were indicated in a

letter to Moylan: "We have in the way . . . of genuine religious
equality . . . the worst obstacle the Devil has ever invented for
the Irish, an *irreligious revolutionary society* in which patriotism takes the form of indifferentism or hostility to religion.
This is the enemy of the Irish cause in our time, and it is that,
every man should combat, first and foremost." McGee went on
to warn that, "Fenianism . . . is not honest men gone astray . . .
but dogmatic, anti-clerical demagogues, strong in their pride
of opinion and eager for propagandism . . . a new sect who aim
at changing the heart and mind of Ireland, i.e., the faith and
feeling of the people, even more than its government. This sect
is altogether novel in Irish history, and it is not to be put down
by half-apologetic pleadings of 'good intentions'."[121] This was
substantially the view taken by Archbishop Cullen, and McGee
would clearly deal with the Fenians in his own time in his own
way.

The *Irish Canadian* referred to McGee as a pretended
patriot and former friend, yet it welcomed McGee's denial of
Brown's statements about the Montreal Fenians and would
have been content to handle him gently had he refrained from
further attacks on the Fenians.[122] Murphy's conciliatory attitude was further indicated by his acceptance of Bishop Lynch's
request not to hold a procession on St. Patrick's Day.[123]

HIBERNIAN "ANNEXATIONISM"

Yet before the impression of Fenian fever had worn off, the
Hibernians began to feel the influence of the second Fenian
convention held in Cincinnati, Ohio, in January 1865. This
was attended by 348 delegates, including two from Canada,
and represented in all 273 circles, an increase of 210 over their
previous Chicago convention. O'Mahony declared that the
Brotherhood was virtually at war with the oligarchy in Great
Britain and, although there was "no Fenian army in the field",
such a force existed: "The Fenian Congress acts the part of a
general assembly of the Irish people." Clerical condemnation
was dismissed as ineffective and hostile clergy were thanked for
the "publicity they gave our association".[124]

Stephens, upon his return to Ireland after his visit to the Fenian Fair at Chicago, had declared that there must be an uprising by 1865 or a dissolution of the organization. Substantial sums were at last being sent to Ireland, and with the American Civil War drawing to a close it was evident that vast numbers of trained military men would come under the direction of the Brotherhood.

In response to the growing enthusiasm of the American Fenians, the Toronto Hibernians could no longer act as an isolated Canadian wing of the movement. Understanding the need for a change of tone, yet realizing the danger of action, Murphy appears to have responded by a new interest in annexation and republicanism. There were signs of this as early as August 1864 when the *Irish Canadian* dismissed Confederation, declaring that it was impossible "to shape the manifest destiny of a people".[125] Early in November 1864 under the heading "British American Nation", the *Irish Canadian* announced that with the restoration of the Union, Canada must cease to be British since the United States "will not tolerate a British American Nation".[126]

As a consolation for not holding a procession on St. Patrick's Day in 1865, the Hibernians invited James MacDermott, a young friend of O'Mahony who later turned informer,[127] to address them on the subject of republicanism. MacDermott offered a somewhat feeble exercise in comparative government which was dismissed contemptuously by the *Globe* and the *Leader*[128] but applauded vigorously at the meeting. A week later the *Irish Canadian* declared for "Annexation to the American Republic on fitting terms and in due season."[129] Similar editorials followed on April 5 and April 12. Annexation was predicted rather than advocated, and republicanism was offered as an improvement over the existing system rather than as a revolutionary alternative. It was not that the Hibernians were dropping their constitutionalist masquerade, but that they were undergoing a change of attitude.

Until the Chicago convention the Hibernians, and even the Fenians who shaped their policy, had somewhat vague notions of what Fenianism was about. With the Cincinnati convention and the end of the American Civil War in April, it was clear that Fenianism was republican and revolutionary, but thus far there had only been hints that Fenian energies might be directed towards an invasion of Canada.

On May 15, 1865, D'Arcy McGee, who had been searching for a chance to make a dramatic and effective declaration against the Fenians, found the means of doing so. In his capacity as Minister of Agriculture and Immigration, he had been sent to represent Canada at the International Exhibition at Dublin. While in Dublin, McGee was invited to address the Young Men's Society at his birthplace in Wexford. Entitling his address, "Twenty Years' Experience of Irish Life in America", he summarized the substance of his social and political ideas as they had matured since leaving Ireland as a republican exile in 1848.[130]

There was little in his speech that he had not said before, and his views differed little from those of the Irish Constitutionalists who supported Archbishop Cullen's National Association. Perhaps McGee's most telling point was that although the Americans shared Irish antipathy for British policy, they did not accept the Irish as social equals in the United States. The Irish were socially and politically the weakest community in the republic. He discouraged emigration "for if wages in North America were higher, life was shorter". McGee dismissed his republicanism of 1848 as "honest folly which had nothing in common with the Punch and Judy Jacobinism of the Fenians", and he declared that he had never seen a "specimen of the genus Fenian in Canada".[131]

As a declaration of war against Fenianism, the speech served well enough, but his use of ridicule and his repudiation of the ideas of 1848 offended former Young Irelanders, including Gavan Duffy, who had been his friend. In sacrificing part of his popularity, he became an easier target for the Fenians. Yet Canadian Fenians were at the moment more concerned with the plans for an uprising in Ireland and the growing schism in the American Fenian movement than they were with McGee.

# CHAPTER FOUR

# The Fenian Schism

A successful rising in the Ireland of the 1860s was impossible, but a vast number of Irishmen on both sides of the Atlantic believed in it. Of these, the Irish veterans of the Civil War, not yet reconciled to civil life, had a special need for a social organization with a military purpose. Such an organization would have equal interest for Irish Americans generally who were attracted by the military and nationalist themes at picnics, dances, and public meetings. The Fenians could meet this need, but in the course of doing so would have to spend much of the money collected for military purposes on the cost of maintaining the social organization they had created.

To sustain the organization, the myth of an imminent rising was sufficient, but there were very few among those who enjoyed the excitement of belonging to a revolutionary club who were willing to take great risks on its behalf. Yet the myth had to be sustained by action, and between 1865 and 1870 various Fenian leaders, because they themselves were believers, were able to provide enough action to keep the myth alive.

Stephens was in the position of a man who would not recognize the impossibility of his enterprise but was always impressed by immediate difficulties. He was under pressure from military men like John Devoy, who had served in the Foreign Legion, and later by Irish American officers who were prepared to act with the forces at hand without much regard for the consequences. Devoy, whose task it was to subvert the British troops in Ireland, claimed that 16,000 out of the 40,000-man garrison had taken the Fenian oath and he was willing to gamble on ordering a mutiny and mass desertion of Fenian soldiers, without waiting to arm the network of Fenian circles.[1] He cited the precedent of the Indian Mutiny, but as there were none of the usual signs which precede a mutiny—insubordination, high incidence of desertion, and military riots—Stephens, wisely perhaps, was unwilling to take the risk. Yet his alternate plan of buying arms in Britain with American money and providing American officers for his underground militia proved impossible.

In his numerous tours of Ireland, Stephens had acquired a vast number of adherents, willing to accept appointments as officers in his network, who had induced a large number of men of military age to take the Fenian oath. These circles held military exercises secretly, in theory, but they tended to become public when there were rumors of an impending uprising. As Ribbon Societies often held drills and parades and O'Connell had organized uniformed bands known as Liberators,[2] participation in this kind of exercise was not conclusive proof of willingness to take part in a rising. There would be no obligation to rise unless the promised arms and officers could be supplied and Stephens, who considered himself a professional revolutionary, would not countenance action without preparation.

All Stephens's moves, like the founding of the *Irish People* in the autumn of 1863, seemed more likely to institutionalize the idea of revolution than to prepare the ground for an immediate rising. The *Irish People*[3] gained a circulation of 8,000 but did not achieve its original purpose of raising money, and although it helped sustain Fenian morale, the information it provided was often useful to the authorities, making the Fenians "felon-setters" against themselves. Moreover, the office of the *Irish People* was watched by the Dublin police and the staff infiltrated by Pierce Nagle who, after gaining the confidence of some American Fenians, offered his services to the British consul in New York.[4]

Not only was Stephens's idea of a large and efficient conspiratorial organization incompatible with secrecy, but the morale of his organization demanded the perpetual anticipation of imminent action which had to be disappointed. Impatient friends and ambitious rivals were ready to accuse Stephens of indecision, cowardice, and even treason, and the need to quiet such opposition probably induced him to commit himself to insurrection or dissolution of the organization in 1865. This provided temporary unity at the price of accepting a deadline which Stephens could not expect to meet.

Until 1865, the American Fenians, who had sent only $45,000 to Ireland since the founding of the organization in 1858, could hardly complain of inaction. Yet with the new affluence of the American movement, O'Mahony, who had always been sceptical about the extent of Stephens's following, despatched a series of agents to Ireland to report on the state of Stephens's forces. Philip Coyne, the first inspector, was followed by Captain T. J. Kelly. Still not satisfied, O'Mahony sent General F. F. Millen, who had acquired his rank serving in the forces of Juarez[5] and who later turned informer against the Fenians. These inspectors were permitted to consult with local leaders and to examine muster rolls and, when they insisted, Stephens arranged a gathering of any Fenian circle they cared to meet. A general inspection was impossible because it would obviously alert the authorities, and Stephens complained that the repetition of these investigations jeopardized the security of his underground militia. All these agents reported favourably on Stephens's claim to have about 80,000 reliable men, a figure which is also supported by the testimony of John Devoy.[6] Yet this seems excessive; Stephens's successors who planned the rising of 1867 thought in terms of 10,000 men.

Stephens estimated that £300,000 would provide small arms for 100,000 men, and 300 cannon, which he believed could be purchased in Britain. Nothing like this could be provided by the American Fenians who raised $228,000 in 1865,[7] of which about $100,000 was sent to Ireland. Yet since much of this was seized by the authorities, Stephens may have received less than $50,000.[8]

Irish American officers who arrived in Ireland at the end of

the Civil War were not difficult to identify, particularly when
they called at the office of the *Irish People*. Many were arrested
and the funds they carried confiscated. Nor does it seem that
Stephens was able to purchase any substantial quantity of
arms with the funds that did reach him. As the summer drew
to a close, his projected uprising was clearly impossible, and
he may have been relieved when the government raided the
office of the *Irish People* on September 15, 1865 on the eve of
the third convention of the American Fenians.[9]

In America, the arrest of Fenian leaders would be accepted
as evidence that there was an underground force about to rise,
and the fact that Stephens was not arrested suggested that the
coming insurrection had prospects of success.[10] This belief
would be a source of strength to O'Mahony, who was resisting
demands of American Fenians that the resources of the organization be directed against Canada. Under pressure from
B. Doran Killian, who once worked for McGee on the *American Celt* and who was now a New York lawyer, O'Mahony had
already agreed to a diversionary raid designed to seize the
island of Campo Bello,[11] later the summer home of the
Roosevelt family, in the hope of securing belligerent status.

The main effort would still be in Ireland, and the Fenians
secured the release of John Mitchel, who was being held as a
Confederate sympathizer, so that he could go to France to take
charge of Fenian funds, henceforth to be sent to Ireland by
way of France. In the course of securing Mitchel's release,
Fenian leaders saw Secretary of State W. E. Seward, and
President Johnson and, with the Campo Bello project in mind,
they secured an ambiguous statement from the President that
he would recognize accomplished facts.[12]

These remarks were conveyed to the six hundred Fenian
delegates meeting in Philadelphia and soon found their way
into the press. Only eighty-two had assembled for the Chicago
convention in 1863, and 348 met at Cincinnati in January
1865,[13] but the organization now could no longer be controlled
by O'Mahony. Although he was re-elected president of the
Brotherhood, a senate of fifteen members was created as a
check on his power.[14] Delegates from each state and district
had elected representatives to the Philadelphia convention and

these in turn nominated the senators, choosing a majority which was hostile to O'Mahony. The senators then elected a president of the senate, who was to become vice-president of the Brotherhood and would control the raising of funds and setting of salaries for Fenian officials. Ultimate power was to reside in the Fenian congress which would include delegates elected from centres on the basis of one delegate for every one hundred paid-up members. The president could choose his cabinet, subject to the approval of the senate. This cabinet would include a secretary of war, an agent of the Irish Republic, a bond agent, and a corresponding secretary.[15] O'Mahony received a salary of $2,000, and three of the secretaries $1,500 each.[16]

One of the first acts of the reconstructed Fenian hierarchy was the renting of the Moffatt Mansion on Union Square, New York, at $1,000 a month, and a payment of $6,000 as security against damages. This was of questionable value for purposes of conspiracy, but the Fenians had by this time become a substantial social and fraternal society whose members would take pride in the visible splendour in which the secretariat was housed.[17] O'Mahony had opposed the acquisition of the mansion, but had yielded to the influence of Brigadier General T. W. Sweeny, the Fenian Secretary of War, who was also a strong partisan of the Canadian project. With such expenditures, it is difficult to credit O'Mahony's statement that only $89,970 out of the $453,000 collected was spent in the United States.[18]

It does not appear that there would have been an immediate schism in the Fenian movement on the question of invading Canada had there not been a dispute about the Fenian bonds which were being sold to finance the Irish uprising and which would be redeemed by the future Irish republic. When the Fenian Bond Secretary, Patrick Kennan, resigned in late November, O'Mahony, unwilling to wait for the meeting of the senate in January, took over the function of Bond Secretary and had his own name engraved on the bond issue. Fearing that O'Mahony intended to take both the function and the salary of the secretary, the senate called an emergency meeting on December 2, 1865. O'Mahony declared the special session illegal and was in turn charged with violating his oath of office and of calumniating the senate and members of the Brotherhood. He replied by accusing the senators of being bribed by British gold to disrupt the movement.[19]

In the ensuing dispute, which was fully reported in the New York press, the Fenians retained the sympathy of the *Herald,* edited by James Gordon Bennett, and the *Tribune,* edited by Horace Greeley, but the *Times* declared that of the money collected by the Fenians "not one tithe is used for any other purpose than maintaining a set of scamps in idleness". Among the Irish papers, the *Freeman's Journal,* reflecting church policy, looked forward to the dissolution of the movement, while the influential *Irish American* took the side of the senate, leaving O'Mahony without an effective defender.[20]

In order to deal with this crisis, O'Mahony called a new Fenian convention which was attended by six hundred delegates and met in New York early in January. At this meeting, the constitution of the Chicago convention was restored. O'Mahony resumed the title of Head Centre and ruled with an executive committee of five. A new journal, the New York *Irish People,* was founded and the convention rejected an appeal for unity offered by General T. W. Sweeny.

Canadian Fenians were represented by Father John Curley and Edward O'Meagher Condon, who had introduced the Brotherhood to Canada but was not a permanent resident of the province. Murphy, who seems to have attended previous conventions, was loyal to O'Mahony but did not attend this convention. Plans for a diversionary raid against Canada were abandoned and the coming uprising was to be in Ireland and "no where else". Throughout the proceedings, a guard of honour from the National Guard protected the meeting from "British spies" and the senate wing of Fenianism.[21]

PROJECTED INVASION OF CANADA

The senate met on January 18 making Roberts president, but instead of calling a convention immediately, it sent Roberts and General Sweeny on a tour of the Eastern and Midwestern centres to advertise the idea of an invasion of Canada. At the first of these gatherings, held at Newark, New Jersey, it proved necessary to eject by force young James MacDermott, a strong supporter of O'Mahony who had addressed the Toronto Hibernians on St. Patrick's Day in 1865. Sweeny declared that he had an invasion plan which he was prepared to submit to any six American general officers for approval, and if they found it unsatisfactory he would adopt any plan they might suggest. In Buffalo, some days later, Roberts called for 100,000 rifles, declaring that 50,000 men in the field would be sufficient to sweep John Bull into the sea. Sweeny added that "If we can get a foothold on which to raise the Irish flag, we shall be recognized."[22]

The tour was followed by a convention which opened in Pittsburgh on February 19, 1866. Sweeny's plan was accepted and a plea for unity from Killian and Father Curley was scornfully rejected. The schism was now complete and it soon became evident that the pro-Fenian section of the American press favoured the Canadian project. The New York *Citizen,* which respected O'Mahony as the founder of the Brotherhood, stated that there was reason to believe that the President of the United States was sympathetic to the invasion, adding, "We bid Head Centre O'Mahony good speed in his early march on Canada." More pointedly, the hostile *Herald* insisted that whatever chance there might have been of a rising in Ireland had passed, but that there was a probability of success in the Roberts–Sweeny plan. The *Herald* editor wrote, "If the Fenians are not prepared to strike anywhere, they had better settle up their accounts . . . and stop their warlike assessments."[23]

These warlike gestures might have attracted the bulk of O'Mahony's supporters had it not been for the news from Ireland. Stephens had been arrested on November 11 and then freed in a spectacular rescue operation on November 24.[24] The suspension of habeas corpus on February 17, 1866 was accepted as evidence that the country was finally in a state of insurrection. An outdoor meeting was called at Jones Wood, near New York, on March 4 which, in spite of the remonstrance of Archbishop John McClosky,[25] attracted a crowd estimated at 100,000. Here they were addressed by Captain John McCafferty who had been arrested in Dublin at the time of the raid on the *Irish People* but had been released by the British authorities because he was a native American. McCafferty spoke of a Fenian army in Ireland, "the best disciplined the world ever knew", that required nothing more than arms which American money could purchase.[26]

The flow of money across the Atlantic had been sustained by O'Mahony, who sent $17,000 to Mitchel during the month of December, in spite of the schism. By March 10, 1866, Mitchel reported having received $46,000.[27] Yet by the middle of March, the arrival in Paris of Irish refugees fleeing after the suspension of habeas corpus made it clear that there would be no rising in the immediate future. Faced with the danger of losing the initiative and fearing that the bulk of American Fenians might turn towards the senate wing, O'Mahony, at a meeting of the Fenian executive council on St. Patrick's Day of 1866, accepted the idea of a diversionary expedition against Canada.[28]

This had originally been the idea of B. Doran Killian who had selected the island of Campo Bello—which at this time was claimed by both Britain and the United States—for an attack. Men were to arrive at Eastport, Maine, without arms or ammunition so that the neutrality law would not be broken. The arms were to arrive by a different route. The Fenians would arm themselves quickly, seize Campo Bello, declare themselves at war with the British Empire, and demand belligerent status. From this base they might either prepare an expeditionary force for landing in Ireland or send out privateers to attack British commerce on the high seas.[29]

O'Mahony's decision to launch a raid against Campo Bello was made within a year after D'Arcy McGee insisted at Wexford that he had "never encountered the genus Fenian in Canada". Then it was still possible to ignore the Canadian Fenians and convenient to do so, and McGee treated Fenianism as an aspect of the corrupting influence of American political institutions. On the eve of the O'Mahony raid, Fenianism

had become a major issue in Canadian politics and the ag-
gressiveness of the Toronto Hibernians made it clear that it
was not entirely an external threat.

In the spring of 1865 the Hibernians had regained a measure
of respectability by adhering to Bishop Lynch's request that
they refrain from outdoor processions on St. Patrick's Day.[30]
It was not a difficult decision to make because the Hibernians
were undoubtedly alarmed by the "Fenian Fever" which had
followed the demonstration of November 4. By the summer
of 1865, the Hibernians were bolder and felt that the Orangemen's insistence upon holding their parade on July 12th gave
the Hibernians a claim to sympathy among liberals and fellow
Catholics.

Bishop Lynch had condemned Fenianism,[31] and often had
been embarrassed by Hibernian extravagances, but he had
never condemned the Hibernian Society. The Hibernians were
therefore inclined to take his tolerance for granted. It was
not easy for a bishop to break openly with an aggressive and
well organized minority which had taken root in his diocese,
and it was particularly difficult for Lynch who had first encouraged the Hibernians and who was himself a strong Irish
nationalist. Bishop John Farrell in the neighbouring diocese
of Hamilton had condemned the local Hibernian Society in
June 1864[32] to prevent it taking root among his flock, but had
hitherto taken no action to prevent Hamilton Catholics from
going to the annual excursions of the Toronto Fenians who
went to Niagara Falls by way of Hamilton.

By mid-July 1865, Bishop Farrell felt the need to reiterate
his position on the Hibernians and did so by warning the
Catholics of Hamilton not to attend the annual excursion.
This warning was apparently effective, for when the excursion
returned to Hamilton Murphy lost his temper and denounced
the bishop for interfering with innocent pleasure. "Such
Saxonized threats" had no authority, whether "uttered by a
Catholic Bishop or by a renegade and a traitor." After this
outburst, Murphy then called for three cheers for the Bishop
of Toronto.[33]

The *Canadian Freeman* immediately noted the insult
to the Bishop of Hamilton and, in a separate article,

warned Irishmen of Adjala and vicinity—the scene of the
Fenian Fever of the previous winter—that Fenians were active
among them and that if they made common cause with the
Fenians, they would injure their religion by encouraging
Orangeism.[34] In the following issue of the *Freeman,* the editor
regretted that opposition to Fenianism would alienate "large
numbers of our friends and supporters". In opposing Fenianism, the editor said he was guided by the example of the church
which condemned the principle of the French and Italian
secret societies with which Fenianism was associated. Fenians
collected money from those who could ill afford it for the sake
of impossible revolutionary schemes. Revolution and conspiracy had done nothing for Ireland, Moylan said, while constitutional agitation had secured tangible gains and could so do
again.[35]

Bishop Lynch now had no choice but to condemn both
Murphy and the Hibernians and apologized to Bishop Farrell
for Murphy's behaviour. In a circular of August 13, 1865,
Lynch condemned the Hibernians, declaring that the Hibernian Society had been established for worthy purposes and had
given no trouble until recently. The bishop went on to say
that Murphy had not responded to previous admonitions and
he now felt obliged to ask all good Catholics to leave the
Hibernian Society.[36]

The Hibernians had difficulty in answering Moylan's contention that Fenianism had done nothing for Ireland, while,
at the same time, convincing their members that they could
ignore the bishop's request. In a leading article in the *Irish
Canadian,* probably written by Boyle, the Fenians were declared to be "the germ of hope, the means of future harvest".[37]
Unintentionally, this touched the heart of the matter. The
North American Fenians felt no need to measure their achievements in terms of tangible improvements in Ireland. It was the
hope or, more precisely, the belief in the coming uprising
which they needed both to sustain the illusion that their
picnics, excursions, and parades were historic occasions, and
to armour them against ridicule. Yet belief in the inevitability
of insurrection in Ireland, Murphy insisted, was not treason
but recognition of a self-evident truth. The hierarchy, the

clergy, and in fact all those who publicly "disagreed with him did so because they feared to express their real beliefs".[38]

In dealing with the bishop's condemnation, the Hibernians began by acknowledging his right to criticize the statements of public men. This apparently was offered as evidence that they accepted the authority of the bishop. At the same time they insisted that Lynch had not given sufficient weight to the provocation that Murphy had suffered at the hands of Bishop Farrell and ended their statement by a declaration of continued confidence in Murphy.[39]

The *Globe* found the bishop's condemnation belated, and complained that Murphy's treasonable utterances had been ignored for years. But this first affront to episcopal dignity brought instant retribution.[40] Bishop Lynch's condemnation would have been more serious for the Hibernians had they not been sustained by rumours of the coming uprising in Ireland.[41] Like the American Fenians, they were prepared to believe that the raid on the office of the *Irish People* was a prelude to a general rising. This was a matter of faith, and to Moylan and McGee a dangerous illusion which separated a part of the Irish community from their fellow Canadians.

Under such headings as "The Fenian Bubble Burst" and "The Beginning of the End" in the *Canadian Freeman*,[42] Moylan sought to shake the confidence of the Hibernians in their interpretation of events in Ireland and at the same time deny that this interpretation was common among Irish Canadians. Yet if Moylan and the Hibernians took opposite views of the events in Ireland, they were both anxious to deny rumours that O'Mahony was planning a diversion against Canada. The *Irish Canadian* could point to the Fenian convention in Philadelphia which firmly denied the existence of such plans,[43] but O'Mahony's plans were known to the Canadian government which called out nine companies of volunteers.[44]

The *Leader* found that an attempt against Canada followed logically from the failure in Ireland[45] and the *Globe* would probably have made a substantial contribution to an invasion scare had the initiative not been taken by the former Orange Grand Master, Ogle Gowan. In a public letter to Nebo Lodge,

Toronto, Gowan advised Orangemen to join the militia to repel the coming invaders and to acquire arms for their personal protection.[46]

This statement was more frightening to liberals than the threatened invasion as Gowan inadvertently raised the question of Orange influence in the militia, which had long been a grievance in the Catholic community. The Fenians were forgotten as the Montreal St. Patrick's Society protested that there were no Catholic officers in the Toronto militia and that many volunteer corps were dominated by Orangemen.[47]

The *Canadian Freeman,* whose editor had no desire to quarrel with Orangemen at that time, found Gowan's "Rampant Loyalty" to be mischievous.[48] Yet the most telling blow was struck by the Grand Lodge of Lower Canada which rebuked Gowan and reasserted its confidence in Catholic loyalty.[49] Gowan undoubtedly had private information about Fenian plans, and as the past champion of an Orange–Catholic alliance he probably had no intention of arousing Catholic animosity. The letter probably had no other purpose than to enhance his position as a public figure and to recover his declining prestige among the Orangemen.

Boyle and Murphy had reason to be grateful to Gowan for distracting attention from the invasion threats, but towards the end of the year they were dismayed by the Fenian schism. It appears to have caught them by surprise. Their first reaction was to insist that since they were not Fenians, they could not presume to express an opinion. They followed this by a statement explaining that the divisions were the result of a conflict of personalities which should be put aside for the general good.[50] When the nature of the split became clear, the Toronto Hibernians immediately declared themselves to be O'Mahony men and undoubtedly were relieved that in doing so they would be taking a stand against all projected invasions of Canada.[51]

Moylan saw in the schism the disintegration of Fenianism which he had predicted in September 1864. What he neglected to take into account was that the schism was a consequence of the rapid growth of the organization at the end of the American Civil War, and that each of the separate wings of American

Fenianism was stronger than the united movement had been at the end of 1863. Apart from that, the tension between O'Mahony and his rivals had inhibited the movement's power to act. The schism left the senate wing free to prepare an invasion of Canada while O'Mahony could, in theory, direct his efforts towards Ireland.

## FENIAN FEVER, MARCH 17, 1866

At the opening of 1866, Moylan commented that the American Fenians had a strong sense of self-preservation, and were content to let the Irish take the risks.[52] Three weeks later he complacently announced that the failure of Fenianism was a vindication of O'Connell's policy of moral force.[53] When Roberts and Sweeny, while on their western tour, threatened invasion, he assured his readers that their plans were "empty gas" and that the United States government would deal promptly with any moves towards British territory.[54] A month later Moylan was mildly apprehensive about the excitement in Montreal and Ottawa over rumours of a Fenian raid into Lower Canada, and insisted that "The Fenian excitement is dying a natural death; sensible people regard it as an empty bubble."[55]

The *Irish Canadian* was inclined towards this view, stating that "Much has been spoken and written on the subject of the Fenian invasion of Canada. From the beginning we looked upon the project (if such was ever intended) as visionary and unproductive."[56] Yet if the Hibernians did not believe in the invasion threats, they were irritated by the expressions of confidence in Catholic loyalty. In a leading article, Boyle wrote, "We are as loyal as we can be," but he asked, "how can the numerous insults of the past years and of the present day be so readily forgotten?"[57] This was written on March 7, the day on which the government called out 10,000 men to guard the frontier against the anticipated invasion. Two days later the *Globe* published reports that raids across the frontier would be co-ordinated with riots in Toronto on St. Patrick's Day, but he asserted confidence in Catholic loyalty.[58]

This was very serious for the Hibernians because Michael

Murphy had announced his intention to hold a procession on St. Patrick's Day. Murphy complained that his renunciation of the parade in 1865 had not been followed by a similar renunciation by the Orangemen on July 12th,[59] but his real motive, as in November 1864, was probably to display his force and give his followers something to do. He had no connection with Roberts's wing, which in any case was not preparing an invasion on St. Patrick's Day, and O'Mahony's decision to seize Campo Bello was not made until March 17, 1866.[60]

Murphy wrote to the *Globe* on March 12 that he was "ignorant of any cause for such apprehended disturbance, and will say for the society over which I preside that they are equally ignorant of apprehended trouble."[61] In its turn, the *Irish Canadian* insisted that there was no real fear of a riot but the "clamour of the press" was designed to wean the Irish from their "affection for their own land".[62]

D'Arcy McGee wrote to Bishop Lynch, advising him to forbid the Catholics to parade,[63] but the bishop was reluctant to take action and asked the governor, Lord Monck, to ban the parade. Monck refused to act[64] and the bishop then issued a pastoral in which he condemned Fenians as lawless men, and reminded Catholics of their duty to defend the frontier against invaders.[65] A much stronger statement by Bishop Farrell declared that "Fenians were not Catholics, being cut off from the Church" and that "O'Mahony was condemned by the Church and despised by society".[66]

The *Globe* considered that Bishop Lynch should have explicitly forbidden the procession, but the Hibernians who had ignored the bishop's condemnation of the Society the previous August would hardly have been influenced by a stronger statement. Moylan insisted that Murphy had the right to hold a procession but that no sensible man would "exercise it under the present circumstances". In a letter to the press, Murphy protested that he intended no trouble, but he could hardly hope to convince the Orangemen.[67]

On March 16, Gilbert McMicken, who acted as chief of the frontier detectives in Canada West, went to see Murphy in Toronto and received assurances that the Hibernians would take pains to avoid provocation, carrying no banners or in-

signia offensive to loyalists; but Murphy also expressed his apprehension about the Orangemen. McMicken in turn assured
a greatly relieved Murphy that the largely Orange militia
would be kept in the armouries on St. Patrick's Day.[68]

When the day arrived, about six hundred Hibernians[69]
marched without the presence of a single clergyman and lis-
tened to speeches by Murphy, Boyle, and others. There were no
serious incidents and Murphy not only praised the Canadian
system but had no fault to find with the "good and energetic
men who ran the government. If some believed that the government across the border was better, that was no concern of
his."[70] To balance this loyalist stance, he announced that there
were 100,000 Irishmen in Canada prepared to take part in the
coming uprising in Ireland.[71]

Meanwhile, on St. Patrick's Day in Montreal the governor
general, Lord Monck, congratulated the Irish Canadians on
their loyalty in what was, in effect, an anti-Fenian demonstration. McGee noticed that two of those present failed to remove
their hats during the singing of "The Queen", but such feeble
gestures merely served to support McGee's contention that
there were few Fenians in Montreal.[72]

On March 21, the *Irish Canadian* dismissed the idea of invasion, declaring that the threats of the Fenian leader, Sweeny,
as far as Canada was concerned were a "mere waste of words
and time".[73] Yet five days earlier O'Mahony had decided to
seize Campo Bello and, in spite of his previous assurances to
the contrary, Murphy would support his action. On April 9
Murphy was arrested along with several of his followers while
en route to Montreal by train. A telegram sent to Murphy in
code informing him of the projected attack on Campo Bello
had been read and deciphered by authorities. When arrested,
Murphy and his companions were carrying revolvers and
$1,000 in cash, yet, as the *Irish Canadian* pointed out on April
18, they had broken no law of the land.

THE CAMPO BELLO FIASCO

Until the senate wing announced its intention of invading
Canada, Fenianism had been little more than a matter of dis-

pute among Toronto journalists and an occasional irritant to
D'Arcy McGee. Early in 1866 the invasion threat made it a
concern throughout the province and, with the concentration
of Fenians in Eastport, Maine,[74] in April, it suddenly became
a concern of the Atlantic provinces precisely when public
opinion there was hardening against Confederation. In February 1865, the pro-Confederation Charles Tupper, the premier of Nova Scotia, considered it inexpedient to make an
issue of Confederation after Leonard Tilley's defeat in New
Brunswick.

The question of Fenianism had already created difficulties
for Thomas Lewis Connolly, the Archbishop of Halifax. Connolly was a friend of John A. Macdonald and D'Arcy McGee.
He had taken a stand against the Fenians in 1864 at the time
of the Toronto Fenian Fever when the Halifax *Burning Bush,*
an ultra-Protestant journal, had declared that Fenians were
storing arms in Catholic churches.[75] When rumours of O'Mahony's first projected diversionary raid against Canada reached
the Maritimes, Connolly had written a widely publicized letter
to Lieutenant-Governor Arthur Gordon of New Brunswick, a
letter which would have done credit to D'Arcy McGee. The
Irish Catholics in the British provinces, he insisted, had nothing to expect from annexation to the United States except
"increased taxation, diminished income, a decided fall in the
social scale and the scathing contempt of their new rulers".
Connolly dismissed the Fenians as "pitiable knaves and fools".
If they invaded Canada they would be treated by both Catholic and Protestant as "freebooters and assassins".[76]

Connolly was a commanding figure in the hierarchy, but
there were no organized Fenians in Nova Scotia, and his strong
views on Fenianism were not echoed by Bishop John Sweeny
of Saint John, New Brunswick, who had spoken publicly
against Confederation.[77] New Brunswick was the key province
in the Confederation project. There the influential St. John
*Morning Freeman,* edited by Timothy Warren Anglin, opposed Confederation and was inclined to treat anti-Fenian
statements with suspicion.[78] There is no evidence of an organized Fenian circle in New Brunswick, but there were undoubtedly individual Fenians, and the long history of tension

between Orangemen and Catholics in the province might have provided fertile ground for a Fenian circle.

An atmosphere of crisis emerged in the Maritimes when the militia was called out on March 17, 1866, but the absence of apparent danger soon led the anti-Confederation leaders to ridicule the Fenian threat as a Confederation hoax.[79] Yet the reports in the American press of Fenian activity could not be dismissed easily. When O'Mahony's followers began to gather on April 9 at Eastport and Calais in the vicinity of Portland, Maine, scepticism disappeared. Their arrival coincided with the efforts of Lieutenant-Governor Gordon to secure the resignation of the anti-Confederation premier, A. L. Smith. For reasons which had little to do with Fenianism, Smith resigned on April 10, leaving the pro-Confederates, led by Tilley, free to exploit the Fenian excitement.[80]

Fenians seemed at this point to be risking more for Canadian Confederation than for Irish independence. Yet there was an element of logic in what the Fenians did. Had they had the advantage of surprise, they might have seized the undefended island of Campo Bello. Although this would not have secured them belligerent status, even a temporary occupation of British territory would increase Fenian prestige. Yet surprise was impossible because the decision to seize Campo Bello, made on March 17,[81] was revealed to the British consul in New York on March 20 by James MacDermott, who had addressed the Toronto Hibernians on the previous St. Patrick's Day. It was possible, then, for Canadian and British authorities to mobilize more force at the threatened point than the Fenians would care to challenge.

H.M.S. *Pylades* was off Campo Bello a day before the Fenians arrived in strength. It could not prevent five Fenians from raiding a customs house on Indian Island and making off with a Union Jack,[82] but Fenian spirits were dampened by the arrival of the eighty-one-gun H.M.S. *Duncan,* carrying over seven hundred British regulars, who joined the U.S.S. *Winooski* off Campo Bello on April 17, the day on which Leonard Tilley formed his new pro-Confederation government in New Brunswick.[83]

On the same day, the *Ocean Spray,* a vessel acquired by the

Fenians from war surplus, arrived at Eastport carrying 1,500 stand of arms and 100,000 rounds of ammunition. The commander of the *Winooski* telegraphed to Washington for instructions, but the American government hesitated to act and the arms were not seized until April 19 when General George C. Meade, the victor of Gettysburg, arrived with three hundred United States troops.[84]

By this time there was not only an American general at the frontier, but also two British generals and a vice-admiral of the fleet. The officer commanding the Maritimes, Major General Sir Hastings Doyle, sailed with the regulars in the *Duncan*[85] while the hero of Kars, Major General Sir Fenwick Williams, the newly appointed lieutenant-governor of Nova Scotia, could not resist hastening to the New Brunswick border.[86] Vice-Admiral Sir James Hope was in command of the naval operations. Somewhat hesitantly, Lieutenant-Governor Gordon sent a cypher telegram to Sir Hastings Doyle asking, "Will not the Fenians bringing a General to the front give them much ground for boasting?"[87]

There were about five thousand British regulars and Canadian militia prepared to act against some four hundred Fenians at Calais, about four hundred at Eastport, Maine, and perhaps another two hundred scattered at Lubec, Pembroke, and Robinson.[88] As it was a question of preventing mischief rather than repulsing invasion, this ratio of about one to five was not excessive, but it was sufficient to restrain the Fenians until their last hopes vanished with the arrival of General Meade.

Fenian propaganda which accompanied this campaign was so well-suited to the needs of the supporters of Confederation that anti-Confederates noted that Killian, the principal author and original sponsor of the expedition, had once been D'Arcy McGee's assistant editor at the *American Celt*. This connection was also noted by some Fenians who suspected that Killian was still working for McGee, and a letter addressed to Killian bearing a forged signature of McGee appeared in the Toronto press at this time.[89]

Killian had a limited knowledge of public opinion in the British American provinces. He understood that there was some republican and annexation sentiment and a substantial body of opinion opposed to Confederation. It therefore made sense to him to offer sympathy to fellow republicans and to help those opposed to Confederation. Speaking in Calais shortly after his arrival there, Killian declared that it was the evident duty of the Fenians to wreck Confederation.[90]

Killian evidently did not realize that what few Canadian republicans there were did not think that changing the system of government was worth an invasion, nor did he understand that once Confederation was identified with loyalty, it was bound to succeed. Timothy Anglin commented that if Killian was in the pay "of the Canadians and Mr. D'Arcy McGee himself wrote the speech for him", he could have rendered no greater service to Confederation.[91]

In Lower Canada *Le Pays,* the Montreal newspaper that expressed the views of the anti-Confederate Parti Rouge, wrote, "Sans l'aide des féniens, les ennemis du gouvernement responsable savent qu'ils ne peuvent rien. Nous avons déjà appelé l'attention sur cette remarquable coïncidence: la déclaration de Killian qu'il savait parfaitement calculée pour aider les unionistes, déclaration pour laquelle, nous n'en doutons pas, il était payé par le parti canadien."[92]

Since Leonard Tilley won a substantial victory in the New Brunswick provincial election in May and Charles Tupper introduced the measures which brought Nova Scotia into Confederation as the troops were leaving for Campo Bello, the fears of Anglin and *Le Pays* were well-founded. Yet it seemed that Fenianism was a bubble after all, and it had burst at Campo Bello.

Stephens arrived in America shortly after the Campo Bello affair. He took over the leadership of the O'Mahony wing, denouncing both the expedition to Maine and the senate wing's projected invasion of Canada.[93] By May 10 Moylan wrote a lengthy obituary on Fenianism in the Toronto *Canadian Freeman,* explaining that its growth was a consequence of the American Civil War and describing its methods of raising money as blackmail. He compared the Fenian leaders to P. T. Barnum.[94]

Under the circumstances, nothing could have been better

suited to the needs of the senate wing of the Fenians which was in earnest about its invasion of Canada. The "Eastport fizzle", as Roberts called it, proved to be an unintentional feint which distracted attention from the preparations which the senate wing was making and tended to discredit all further reports of invasion projects.

CANADIAN SECURITY

Up to this time, British and Canadian intelligence work had been effective. As the Fenians in the earlier days of the movement proved a threat to the British administration in Ireland rather than Canada, the Fenians were originally the concern of the British minister in Washington and British consuls in key cities like New York and Buffalo. When the first signs of a serious threat towards Canada appeared, responsibility for Fenian surveillance fell to Gilbert McMicken, stipendiary magistrate at Sarnia, who controlled a force of detectives in Upper Canada which had been organized to deal with American Confederate agents and sympathizers operating on Canadian territory.[95]

There was at this time no permanent secret service, and confidential agents were employed by various departments of government as the need arose. Apart from this, British diplomats and Canadian ministers were deluged with unsolicited reports of an alarmist nature and occasional offers by Fenians to provide information for money. The latter, if they seemed plausible, were contacted, and as a rule proved quite useful.

Because of the improbable nature of Fenian projects and the exaggerated reports of their numbers in the press and in letters of self-appointed informants, British agents were reluctant to believe that the Fenian leaders were in earnest about their invasion plans and were inclined to seek other explanations for Fenian activities. At the time of the Chicago convention in November 1863, the British consul at Buffalo wrote that the object of the Fenians was to mobilize the Irish vote for the coming presidential election.[96] J. E. Wilkins, a special agent employed to investigate Fenianism, wrote in August 1865 that the publicity given the Fenians was the result of the disorganized state of the Irish vote which had formerly been given to the Democratic party but was now being courted by the Republicans. According to Wilkins, the Republicans were hoping to counter the feelings aroused against them by conscription by offering expressions of sympathy towards Irish nationalism. Wilkins also insisted that the Fenians did not command the support of the entire Irish American community.[97]

The principal burden of Fenian surveillance fell upon Edward Archibald, the British consul in New York. Archibald was a Nova Scotian of North Irish ancestry who had a flair for intelligence work. His most important task was to select useful agents from the various Fenians who offered their services. His code name for informers was Mr. Richard,[98] among whom were Pierce Nagle, the agent who had infiltrated the office of the *Irish People* in Dublin, and James "Red" MacDermott, O'Mahony's confidant, who provided Archibald with precise information about the Campo Bello expedition. This information, forwarded to Sir Frederick Bruce, the British minister in Washington, enabled Bruce to take up the matter of the Fenian project with Secretary of State Seward who promised to enforce the neutrality laws.[99]

At the beginning of 1865, the combination of Fenian excitement in Toronto and the Cincinnati convention induced John A. Macdonald to call out two thousand volunteers to impress the Fenians and the United States government with the will of the Canadian people to protect their frontier. Yet he had little apprehension of serious difficulties[100] and, as stated previously, was more worried about the security of the Catholic population than about the security of the frontier. By September, with the vast increase in Fenian strength and convincing rumours that recent arrests in Ireland would be followed by attacks on Canada, Macdonald authorized McMicken to employ six men to watch the Fenians. McMicken decided to place two at Sarnia, two at Goderich, one at Fort Erie, and one at Clifton. He already had men at Cincinnati and Chicago.[101] Shortly afterwards, Sir John Michel, Commander of the Forces in Canada, wrote to Macdonald explaining that his five thousand regulars could not effectively protect the frontier and he asked what force the provinces could place at his disposal if a body of Fenians were to cross the frontier at Niagara or Detroit.[102]

Michel wrote a week later to the British secretary of war, commenting, "I hardly think after the burst of the Irish Fenian bubble that they will make any attempt against Canada, but still, so serious might be the eventualities of a collision with American subjects" that he considered precautions necessary, pointing out that an advance of five or ten thousand men across the frontier could do considerable damage.[103]

D'Arcy McGee took the threat more seriously, inducing Macdonald to send a special agent, R. N. Scott, to New York to observe the Fenians. Scott provided interesting material on Fenian bond issues and discussed the Fenian question with Archbishop McClosky of New York.[104] Yet the most useful work was still being done by Archibald, who summarized his information on Fenianism in a report to the Commander of the Forces at the time of the Philadelphia convention. He declared that the recent arrests had defeated Fenian efforts in Ireland and that in order to sustain their morale they would attack Canada. He attributed the publicity being given the Fenians in the American press to the coming state elections, but a raid of some kind was to be expected.[105]

Yet the governor general of Canada, Lord Monck, was "not apprehensive of anything serious arising from their [the Fenians] proceedings", and complained that he was being pelted with information on the subject; but he agreed that precautionary measures were necessary.[106]

Early in December 1865 Alexander Tilloch Galt, the Canadian finance minister, went to see the American secretary of state, but came away with nothing but assurances that the Fenians were not in earnest about invading Canada and that the neutrality laws would be enforced if they did.[107] Meanwhile, Archibald sent an agent to the New Brunswick frontier in December but found no evidence of Fenian activity.[108] There seemed to be no reason to supplement Archibald's efforts by independent Canadian action in the United States, but his report that thousands of Toronto Fenians were prepared to move at the first sign of a raid across the border required local investigation. This was carried out by McMicken's agent, Patrick Nolan, a former Hibernian, who reported that there were about 650 Hibernians in the Toronto area, not half of them Fenian, and that no trouble was to be expected before the middle of March.[109]

Nolan's report concerning Fenian numbers, which contrasted with rumours coming from New York, was reassuring and confirmed the impression that the Fenians were unlikely to go beyond threats. In the months that preceded the Canadian invasion, there was no want of reliable reports, although these related more to O'Mahony's supporters than to the more dangerous senate wing. In February 1866 there were reports from Buffalo that arms were being stored for the invasion planned for the last weeks in May, and apparently Patrick O'Day, a Buffalo auctioneer, told a private gathering of Fenians that he would give $1,000 for the head of D'Arcy McGee.[110]

By degrees, precautions were taken, although it was not until April that a fleet of nine armed steamers was authorized for service on the Great Lakes, and in the same months four regiments of regulars were ordered to British North America.[111] These precautionary measures were supported by an increasingly efficient intelligence service that enabled the British minister in Washington to tell the American secretary of state where the Fenians were storing arms along the border. General Meade was sent to investigate and arms were seized at Buffalo, Dunkirk, and Rouses Point.[112] Yet while there was evidence of Fenian plans and ability to strike, there was a disinclination to believe that the Fenians still had the will to strike.

On May 17, 1866, McMicken, in whom Macdonald placed a good deal of confidence, reported that he could not conceive of Sweeny making "any demonstration against Canada now" and that there was no indication of a movement of any kind "unless we take the absence of bluster and the unusual quiet everywhere as an indication".[113]

This opinion was supported by Hemans, the British consul

at Buffalo, who wrote on May 19 that Fenianism was "virtually dead" and that the possibility of a raid would hardly justify the maintenance of a costly detective force. A week later, Hemans wrote that the United States deputy marshal had information that a raid from Buffalo had been planned, but that the Americans thought it best to let the "wild and impossible project die a natural death" rather than give the Fenians a reason for ascribing their failure to official interference.[114] John A. Macdonald was already convinced that the "row between Stephens and Sweeny" had put an end to the whole affair, yet he still felt that the Fenians "must be watched".[115]

Although Archibald, Hemans, and McMicken were diligent in acquiring information about the Fenians, they had apparently acquired a somewhat limited insight into Fenian mentality. This apparent disarray of Fenian forces, the improbability of their designs, and the disposition to believe that Fenianism was mere bluster induced a mood of complacency that gave the Fenians the advantage of surprise. The security authorities attached too little importance to the fact that while O'Mahony's sudden decision to seize Campo Bello was supported by an improvised force of a few hundred men, Roberts's wing had been planning and organizing for several months the movement of over ten thousand men. Moreover, the surveillance men failed to perceive that Fenian bluster was combined with audacity and that the experienced officers who commanded the senate forces had no reluctance to take risks.

## THE INVASION OF 1866

General Sweeny's plan of invasion was optimistic, based on an analysis of Canadian history and politics which must have been formed without a study of the War of 1812 or the contemporary Canadian press. In his report to the convention, he stated, "From the opposition of the people of the Eastern Province we have nothing to apprehend. They were positively neutral during the invasions of 1775 and 1812, and the arrogance of British troops has only embittered the aversion which, as Frenchmen, they have always felt toward the conquerors of their forefathers." With regard to Canada West, he pointed out, "The garrisons are small and widely separated, and even the sympathy of their friends, the Orangemen, will be of little real avail when cut off from all assistance from without. They must remain in their fortified towns, until compelled to surrender in detail."[116]

This view, which a reading of the *Irish Canadian* might have corrected, was apparently encouraged by small groups of Fenians in Canada who supported Roberts's wing. Richard Slattery, who headed a Fenian Circle formed on May 8 in Quebec City, wrote the next day to Sweeny:

Everything is progressing rapidly in this district. . . . I have already about 50 volunteers and nearly 100 who are not volunteers, and before Sunday the number will be largely increased. The excitement is all over and the "loyal" inhabitants are no longer haunted in their dreams by visions of Fenian armies. To-night we have a secret meeting of the leading men, when business of importance will be transacted.

There are about 1000 regulars in this garrison, including artillery. There is no cavalry, with the exception of a few volunteer companies. If the General should have any further orders for me, my address is P. Browne, Esq., Daily Murcury [*sic*] Office, Quebec, C. E. Anything addressed as above will reach me safely, and no danger of its being opened or delayed.[117]

General Sweeny had declared at the Pittsburgh convention that he would require ten thousand men and three batteries of artillery with two hundred rounds per man and five hundred per gun.[118] It was assumed that a year's preparation would be needed, but news of Killian's attempt at Campo Bello brought demands for immediate action.[119] As there was no time to raise the $450,000 which Sweeny had originally expected, he had to be content with $100,000. The purchase of artillery proved impossible but several thousand stand of arms were acquired and stored within reach of the frontier.

At the end of May, Brigadier General W. F. Lynch was ordered to take command of the Fenian contingent gathering in the vicinity of Buffalo, which was designated the centre of the Fenian army. A second concentration around St. Alban's, Vermont, including a substantial contingent of cavalry, formed the right wing. The left wing, commanded by Charles C. Tevis, Sweeny's adjutant-general, was based in Chicago.

General Sweeny's[120] plans were designed for an invasion by conventional forces rather than Fenian militia, and it is not surprising that they achieved nothing but the concentration at Buffalo and Vermont which made possible excursions across the frontier. The attack in the west was the most complicated. A contingent from Chicago and Milwaukee, moving by lakes Michigan and Huron, was to take Stratford, and then seize London. Twenty-four hours later, two other contingents were to cross Lake Erie, one concentrating at Port Stanley and moving on to London, the other concentrating at Port Colborne and taking Paris, Guelph, and Hamilton. This threat in the west was intended to force the Canadian defence forces to concentrate on Toronto, leaving Montreal exposed to attack from the Fenian right and centre.

Meanwhile, Canadian Fenians were to destroy the bridge at Ste. Anne de Bellevue, cutting Montreal off from Upper Canada. Contingents were collected south of Prescott and Cornwall to create a diversion. At the same time Brigadier General Murphy, commanding the Fenian cavalry, would move up both sides of the Richelieu River and seize and if possible hold Victoria Bridge which connected Montreal to the south shore of the St. Lawrence. If and when these threats were repulsed, the cavalry was to concentrate on Sherbrooke, which would serve as Fenian headquarters and possibly as capital of the Irish republic in exile.

The western movement of Fenians collapsed when the Michigan rail and boat companies refused to transport them. Brigadier General Tevis could do nothing, and Brigadier General Lynch did not appear in Cleveland to command the projected movement across the lake. As Lynch still had not arrived by May 29, Lieutenant-Colonels John O'Neill and Owen Starr moved their forces to Buffalo. With Lynch still missing on May 31, Sweeny's representative in Buffalo put

O'Neill in command and ordered him to move his forces across the frontier.

An advance party of Fenians marched a few miles north of Buffalo and crossed over to the Canadian side shortly after midnight on May 31. They were followed by O'Neill and the main body of Fenians at 3:30 in the morning. The Fenians occupied Fort Erie, a village of about six hundred, just opposite Buffalo. This village was connected by rail with Ridgeway on the Lake Erie side and with Chippawa where the Welland River flows into the Niagara, not far from Navy Island, where Mackenzie had established his "Canadian Republic" in 1837.

The Fenians found that the rolling stock had been removed from the railway yard at Fort Erie and, since local farmers had driven away or hidden their horses, they could find only enough horses for a small force of mounted scouts. Yet they proceeded to destroy the railway bridge connecting Fort Erie with Ridgeway and to cut the telegraph line. As they had no commissariat of their own, the Fenians laid the town under contribution to feed their forces. General Sweeny's proclamation was published, declaring that they were "here neither as murderers, nor robbers for plunder and spoliation . . . that they were present as an Irish army of liberation". The hand of friendship was offered to Irishmen, Frenchmen, and Americans. Canadians and British were not mentioned unless they were presumed to be under the heading of "Americans".[121]

The main Fenian camp was located at Newbeggin farm, about six miles north of Fort Erie and a mile inland from the Niagara River. Here, on the afternoon of June 1, O'Neill learned that the American gunboat, U.S.S. *Michigan,* had cut off further reinforcements and that two Canadian columns were moving in his direction, one from Chippawa and the other from the south along Lake Erie.

Deciding to deal with the Canadian columns separately, before they united, O'Neill broke camp during the night and marched south in the general direction of Ridgeway. As the failure of Canadian intelligence sources had given O'Neill the advantage of surprise, it was impossible for Canadian authorities to prepare in advance the kind of forces which acted as a deterrent to the Fenian venture at Campo Bello. Moreover, as

Campo Bello was an island, forces could be moved there
quickly by sea. In order to defend an extensive land frontier
threatened at various points, railway would have to be used to
transport the defence forces and, as the regulars available were
limited, much of the burden of defence would fall on the
Canadian militia which would have to face Fenian invaders
commanded by experienced officers.

The Canadian militia had profited by the invasion scare of
March 17 which served as a rehearsal for the real invasion in
June, and the quality of leadership had been improved by the
military schools established by the Canadian government and
staffed by imperial officers.[122] Responsibility for the defence of
Upper Canada rested with Major General George Napier who
maintained his headquarters in Toronto. He received news of
O'Neill's movements at six o'clock on the morning of June 1
from Hemans, the British consul at Buffalo.[123]

The forces immediately available — six companies of regulars and a battery of artillery — were moved to St. Catharines
under the command of Lieutenant-Colonel George Peacocke.
Receiving news that the Fenians were moving north along the
Niagara River, Peacocke proceeded to Chippawa to head off
possible moves towards the locks of the Welland Canal. At the
same time, a force of nine hundred militiamen under Lieutenant-Colonel Alfred Booker, whose second-in-command was
Lieutenant-Colonel J. S. Dennis, was sent from Dunnville to
Port Colborne. As neither of these columns had a force of
mounted scouts, they had to rely on rumours and guesswork in
interpreting Fenian movements.

On the morning of June 2, when O'Neill was proceeding
south towards Ridgeway, Peacocke assumed that he was still at
Newbeggin farm. With this in mind, Peacocke ordered Booker
to proceed by rail to Ridgeway and to take a road leading
north to unite with Peacocke's forces at Stevensville, about five
miles north of Ridgeway and about three miles southwest of
the supposed Fenian encampment.

Before receiving Peacocke's orders, Booker and Dennis had
planned to approach Fort Erie from the west and had sent a
steamer, manned by the Welland Canal Battery and the Dun-
ville Naval Brigade, to patrol the Niagara, thus cutting off the

Fenian line of retreat. Instead of obeying orders at once, Booker sent Dennis ahead in the steamer and telegraphed to Peacocke, requesting a change of plan. Peacocke repeated his original order and by five o'clock Booker's force was moving by train towards Ridgeway.

Booker reached Ridgeway at six o'clock where he was told by local inhabitants of the approach of O'Neill's forces, but having no mounted force to investigate, he ignored this information and marched north for the expected rendezvous with Peacocke at Stevensville. The militia was led by Number Five Company of the Queen's Own Rifles, armed with Spencer repeating rifles, and followed by the rest of the forces, carrying muzzle-loading Lee Enfields. These included Number Seven Company, made up of students of the University of Toronto.

Fenian mounted scouts had heard the whistle of the train approaching Ridgeway and the bugles of the mounted scouts brought news to O'Neill who promptly ordered his forces to take up a position on Limestone Ridge, an elevation of about thirty-five feet, some three miles north of Ridgeway. Earthworks were thrown up and there O'Neill awaited the arrival of the militia.

The advance guard of the Queen's Own was fired on by the Fenian outposts at about 8:30 in the morning. The militia deployed and took cover and after approximately an hour's fighting had driven the Fenians towards their main entrenchment. By this time, the Fenians were low on ammunition. O'Neill was contemplating a withdrawal when the sight of Fenian mounted scouts convinced the Canadian militia that they were about to be attacked by cavalry. Booker accepted the rumour as fact. In anticipation of a cavalry attack, he ordered his men to fall back and form square. This command threw his forces into confusion. Some presented easy targets for Fenian rifles as they tried to change formation. Others mistook the order for a general retreat and a good many simply fled.

Although the militia, as shown by the first hour of the engagement, were equal in courage to the Fenians, like many receiving their baptismal fire they had difficulty in distinguishing between a real and an imaginary danger. O'Neill's veterans took immediate advantage of the militia's confusion and drove them from the field with a bayonet charge.

Peacocke's column heard the sound of gunfire at Ridgeway but was too far away to intervene. Still having no mounted scouts for reconnaissance and in expectation of a battle on the morning of June 3, Peacocke encamped. O'Neill, seeing that he was faced with superior forces, decided to fall back on Fort Erie. Meanwhile, the force under Dennis, which had been sent by steamer along the Niagara, seized Fort Erie. With the approach of the Fenian column withdrawing from Ridgeway, they took shelter behind improvised defences, but were soon overwhelmed by the retreating Fenians. The Fenians thus secured their line of retreat from British and Canadian forces, but still had to reckon with American forces. In the course of the night, they attempted to withdraw across the river in mud scows towed by tugboats and while doing so they were intercepted by the American authorities.[124]

By this time, General Ulysses S. Grant had passed through Buffalo and General Meade, who had dispersed the Fenians at Eastport, had given orders to cut off supplies and seize Fenian arms and ammunition. On June 6, three days after the Fenians had been intercepted and six days after they crossed the Canadian border, President Andrew Johnson issued a proclamation denouncing the Fenians for "high misdemeanours, forbidden by the laws of the United States".[125] With this belated proclamation ended the hopes held by thousands of Fenians concentrated along the frontier of benefiting from the benevolent neutrality of the United States government.

There remained the Fenian efforts against Lower Canada, the most ambitious of all Fenian efforts but the least likely to succeed because of the concentration of British regulars and Canadian militia in the Montreal area. Apart from this, General Meade commenced seizing Fenian stores of arms before the neutrality proclamation, and Fenian senior officers, including General Sweeny himself, were arrested on the night of June 6.[126]

In the face of this vigorous action there was no reason to

expect further raids across the frontier. Consequently the
Fenians again enjoyed the advantage of surprise when Brigadier General Samuel Speer managed to gather about him a
force of one thousand partly armed men and crossed the
Lower Canadian frontier on June 7. In theory he might have
hoped for a second Ridgeway as he seized the small village of
Pigeon Hill, about a mile from the border just east of
Missisquoi Bay and sent a detachment of Fenian cavalry to
skirmish with the defenders of Frelighsburg. By the morning
of June 8, the Fenians occupied four small villages, Pigeon
Hill, St. Armand, East Stanbridge, and Frelighsburg, the
latter three within a five-mile radius of Pigeon Hill. From the
beginning, the position was impossible and Speer had some
difficulty keeping his hungry men from looting as local inhabitants fled from the occupied area.[127]

Speer remained on Canadian soil overnight and in the
morning evacuated St. Armand, which at noon on June 9 was
occupied by a column of regulars and militia. The Fenians
took up a defensive position at Pigeon Hill, but were gone
before the arrival of the Montreal Troop of Guides, which
chased a retreating Fenian column over the border, taking a
few prisoners. By this time the Fenian mounted troops had
already fled and General Speer soon surrendered to the
American border authorities. There were no fragments of
glory to redeem this episode, which was much like the Eastport
fiasco, but after Ridgeway none were necessary.

# CHAPTER FIVE

# Fragmentation and Failure of Fenianism

Since the June raid impressed American and world opinion with the resources and determination of the Fenian movement and convinced Fenian sympathizers that Fenian leaders were in earnest, the effort was not a complete failure. The Fenians had held British territory for over forty-eight hours, had defeated Canadian militia at Ridgeway, and could ascribe their own failure to the intervention of American authorities. The immediate reaction of American opinion to the June raid was negative, but no more so than that of James Stephens who arrived in America just after the Eastport affair. Stephens denounced the June raid as murder. The Canadians, he declared, "were an industrious and inoffensive people . . . blessed with self-government and all the freedom their hearts can desire. . . . Had Ireland the freedom and rights possessed by Canada, he could never have lifted his voice against the British government."[1]

Yet the negative American reaction would be temporary as the "Radical Republicans", who opposed President Johnson's moderation towards the defeated southern states, were prepared to bid for the Fenian vote in the coming congressional election. This cost them very little because there was no Anglophile vote in America, but it would not be easy to break the traditional Democratic loyalties of the Irish Americans.

In theory, James Stephens supported the action of the
Johnson administration in enforcing American neutrality
against the Canadian raid, but he wanted American intervention on behalf of Fenians arrested in Ireland. Consequently,
the supporters of Stephens had their own quarrel with the
administration and, like the Roberts wing, threatened the
president with the hostility of the Irish American electorate.[2]
Under these circumstances, it is not surprising that the
Johnson administration gave ground. Moreover, Seward, the
secretary of state whom the Fenians denounced as the "American Castlereagh", hoped to exploit the Fenian threat to induce
the British government to accept responsibility for the depre-
dations of the Confederate commerce raider, the *Alabama,*
and other raiders that had sailed from British ports[3] during
the Civil War. Seward was a believer in Manifest Destiny,
which he advanced by the purchase of Alaska, but he was
prepared to let the "forces of history" do their work without
the aid of the Fenians.[4]

The main concern of the Roberts wing of Fenianism after
the Canadian raid was the fate of the prisoners held in Canada.
At first the American press was inclined to let Canadian
justice take its course, but the raid was later treated as a mis-
guided effort to secure redress of legitimate Irish grievances.[5]
It is not surprising, then, that Canadian opinion, led by the
*Leader* and the *Globe,* insisted that Canadian courts resist
all external pressure exercised on behalf of the prisoners.[6] The
Bleu journal, *La Minerve,* probably reflected the feeling of the
majority of French Canadians when it declared: "Le Canada
avait des sympathies naturelles pour l'Irlande; tout les deux
pays catholiques unis par les mêmes liens à une domination
protestante. . . . Les Irlandais ont été reçus ici comme des
frères. . . . Les Irlandais ont donc montré une conduite
insensée en se séparant des alliés que la nature et la religion
leur assignaient. Ils ont tourné leurs armes meurtrières contre
ceux qui les ont reçus nus, misérables et afflamés."[7]

The tone of the Rouge *Le Pays* was not very different. "Les
féniens se cachent du soleil pour exécuter leurs projets; ils
violent la neutralité. Ils attaquent le Canada que ne leur a
rien fait, et vous voulez que nous ne nous révoltions pas contre

cette tactique de guérilleros, de filibustiers, de brigands!"[8]

The *Irish Canadian* found that "there cannot be a question but that the movement into Canada was connived at by the American government . . . and that Secretary of State Seward lent himself to the plans of General Sweeny for purposes strictly American." It also stated "for the benefit of our Orange friends . . . that the leaders of the present invasion—Roberts and Sweeny are Protestants." The editor was also pleased to report that of the sixty Fenian prisoners, eighteen were Protestants and one a Scottish born Episcopal clergyman.[9] While repudiating the invasion, the editor of the *Irish Canadian* opposed the suspension of habeas corpus on the grounds that it would put power into the hands of Orange magistrates. Moylan and McGee may have shared these fears, but the *Canadian Freeman* took much the same attitude as the *Leader* and supported the suspension of habeas corpus. In a letter published in the *Canadian Freeman*, McGee refused a request of an old acquaintance to intervene on behalf of a Fenian prisoner. In his letter, McGee insisted that "this filibustering is murder, not war".[10]

At the opening of the Fenian trials in October 1866, the *Canadian Freeman* found that a "revengeful spirit demands capital punishment, mercy is expedient and . . . the country was in a position to deal leniently with the prisoners."[11] Yet disputes about the fate of the prisoners cannot be taken at face value because justice in trials of this kind followed a pattern understood by most participants. At the trials of Fenians on both sides of the Atlantic, leading Fenians would be condemned to death or to long periods of penal servitude. There would be a stay of execution, commutation of the death sentences, and a release of all prisoners when the excitement had subsided. There were no executions in Ireland and all Canadian prisoners were released by 1872.[12] Had the American Fenians not renewed their preparations for raids on Canada, the prisoners in Canada would probably have been released much sooner.

In the course of the trials, the *Irish Canadian* was able to call attention to two points which were taken up by Moylan's *Canadian Freeman*. The first was not directly connected with the trials as it had to do with the Protestant character of the Toronto militia. The *Irish Canadian* as early as 1864 had complained about the absence of Catholic officers in the militia and attributed this to Orange influence.[13] It followed from this that few Catholics came forward to join Protestant-officered units and those who did were often subjected to insults from the Orange rank and file. Militia companies sometimes shouted insults when passing the Bishop's Palace[14] and militia units were at times ordered to attend Protestant church services. The *Canadian Freeman* called attention to the case of J. J. Landry, a Catholic lawyer serving in the militia, who was refused permission to fall out when his company was ordered to attend a Protestant church parade.[15]

A few weeks later, the *Freeman* complained that "certain volunteer companies" in the city were demanding the execution of the Fenian prisoners. The *Freeman* declared that "men armed and clothed at public expense should not seek to dictate to the government."[16]

Following on the heels of the *Freeman*'s complaint, a Protestant clergyman arrested during the raids, D. F. Lumsden, was acquitted, while Father John MacMahon, a Catholic priest, was convicted by a Protestant jury. Both had pleaded innocent but neither had a plausible explanation of their presence among the Fenian raiders.[17] As no Orangemen were on the jury, the *Freeman* insisted that Irishmen of both denominations were being kept off juries. "Orangemen," it declared, "are, after all, Irishmen, and have Irish hearts, and bigotry does not steel their hearts and render them callous to all human sympathy and mercy."[18] Father MacMahon was of course in no danger of his life, although Roberts had looked forward to having MacMahon become a martyr and did not hide his disappointment when his sentence was commuted.[19]

The case of Michael Murphy was overshadowed by the June raids, but was most embarrassing to the government since his presence on a train bound for Montreal was not sufficient to prove his intention of joining the Eastport Fenians. John A. Macdonald had intended to keep him under observation, but Alexander Galt and George Etienne Cartier, acting independently, ordered him arrested at Cornwall.[20] Murphy and his companions resolved this dilemma by escaping from the Cornwall prison on the eve of their trials, and Murphy spent the rest of his days as a tavern-keeper in Buffalo.

The trials of the Fenians taken near Pigeon Hill were held in the relative quiet of Sweetsburg in Lower Canada. They attracted little attention apart from some unfavourable comment in the Toronto *Globe* because only three were condemned to death.[21]

## FENIAN PRESSURE ON THE JOHNSON ADMINISTRATION

Meanwhile, the Johnson administration at Washington, which had been thanked by the British government for its firmness in June, was, in the face of coming elections, giving ground to Fenian pressure. Early in July the House of Representatives defeated a motion for extending belligerent rights to the Fenians almost on the same day that Roberts declared at a public meeting in Buffalo that the Fenian vote would go to those who proved themselves friends of Ireland.[22] Shortly after this, a measure for amending the neutrality laws passed in the House of Representatives, although it was later thrown out by the Senate.[23] Defeat of such legislation was of little concern to its authors as voting for it was sufficient to conciliate the Fenian vote. Nor did the ultimate defeat of the bill unduly disturb Roberts, as the fact of its being discussed by Congress could be offered as evidence of Fenian influence.

More serious were resolutions demanding that the prosecution of the Fenians held for violating neutrality laws be dropped, and demands that the president intervene on behalf of the Fenian prisoners held in Canada. To try to force the president's hand in this matter, Fenians held a public meeting in Washington at the end of July. As in the case of the Hunters in 1839, the Fenians were refused the use of public buildings, and it is a measure of their influence that their friends in Congress intervened to secure for them the use of the National Fair building.[24]

With the adjournment of Congress in August, the president
dropped proceedings against the Fenians arrested in the United
States, forcing the Radical Republicans to bid higher for
Fenian support. Governor Oglesby of Illinois described
President Johnson as a friend of the English government and
publicly regretted the traditional Irish attachment to the
Democratic party.[25] Such utterances received mixed reception
in the largely Democratic Irish American press, and the Democratic New York *Herald* did not hesitate to point out the
previous hostility of the Radicals to the Irish.[26] As John
Mitchel put it, "The Radicals had used Irish bayonets to
crush the South and now wished to use their ballots to keep
the South crushed."[27]

Meanwhile, supporters of Roberts had been re-enacting the
Battle of Ridgeway at Fenian picnics and, in September, at a
convention held at Troy, New York, they reaffirmed their
intention to try a second raid across the frontier.[28] Roberts
announced that their treasury contained $136,000 and that
28,000 stand of arms were in the possession of his followers.
To these were soon to be added arms seized by American
authorities in June, for, as the November election approached,
President Johnson decided to return the arms to the Fenians.[29]
Moreover, the United States government retained a Toronto
lawyer as counsel to those Fenian prisoners who claimed
American citizenship.[30] Throughout the election period, which
ended on November 6, 1866, the Fenians continued their
pressure on the administration to take action on behalf of the
prisoners in Canada.

The Radical Republicans won the election by a substantial
majority, leaving Johnson with a hostile Congress which was
to begin impeachment proceedings against him. The Fenian
vote played its part in this defeat, particularly in New York
State, but the decisive Republican victory gave the party an
independence of the Irish vote. Moreover, with the election
and the trials of Fenians in Canada over, attention shifted
from the Roberts wing towards James Stephens and his plans
for an uprising in Ireland.

Mitchel had grave doubts about Stephens's ability to lead
an American movement and he warned O'Mahony against

giving him the leadership.[31] Stephens obviously lacked abilities
as a demagogue and had cultivated the art of conspiracy rather
than the art of publicity which was essential in the American
movement. Yet there was no other leader with sufficient
prestige to command what had been the O'Mahony wing of
Fenianism. Still, Stephens was an effective if not gifted public
speaker who could hold the attention of crowds attracted by
his reputation. Moreover, he at once seized the initiative by
announcing that there would be an uprising at the beginning
of the new year. This was sufficient to rally about him energetic and able leaders like Colonel Thomas Kelly and the fierce
captain, John McCafferty, who supported the idea of rebellion
in Ireland. However, in making this announcement, Stephens
alarmed the authorities in Ireland who began arresting sus-
pects and searching for arms, thus eliminating any possibility
there had been of launching a serious uprising.[32]

In spite of this, Stephens was able to hold the attention of
his American followers, and at the same time secure a measure
of independence from Irish American officers by obtaining the
services of General Gustave Paul Cluseret.[33] This officer, part
mercenary and part republican crusader, had begun his military career in the French army. He served for a time with
Garibaldi, and had risen to the rank of general in the federal
forces during the American Civil War. In order to pay the required retainer for Cluseret's services, the Fenians had to sell
the *Ocean Spray,* their one substantial asset after the Campo
Bello venture. Cluseret agreed to take command of Fenian
forces when and if the Fenians could provide him with ten
thousand armed men. The plan was to prevent concentration
of Crown forces in Ireland by disrupting railway communications and to stop the arrival of reinforcements by seizing ports.
When this had been done, it was expected that the population
would rally around the original ten thousand Fenian soldiers
and crush the British forces in detail.[34]

Cluseret had doubts about the ability of the Irish Fenians to
put ten thousand men in the field, but like the inspectors
whom O'Mahony had sent to Ireland in 1864, he was impressed by the apparent size of Stephens's movement and the
determination of his followers. Yet he realized that they were

virtually unarmed, and Fenian finances did not permit the extensive purchase of arms.[35] Stephens understood this too, but his immediate need of Cluseret's prestige outweighed the probability that Cluseret would refuse to take command at the eleventh hour.

Indeed, as the eleventh hour approached, Stephens abandoned his somewhat luxurious quarters in the Metropolitan Hotel in New York and went into hiding from his own followers. Towards the end of December, he had to face them and insist that the date of the rising in Ireland be postponed again. In the disputes that followed, Captain John McCafferty threatened Stephens's life and Stephens was deposed as Fenian Chief.[36]

NEW PHASE OF FENIANISM

With the opening of the new year, Fenians entered a new phase. Stephens and O'Mahony were gone, soon to be followed by Roberts,[37] who was to make his way in Democratic politics as congressional representative for New York. The Roberts wing would soon be led by the hero of Ridgeway, General John O'Neill, while Stephens's title of Chief Organizer of the Irish Republican Brotherhood would go to Brigadier General John M. Gleeson, but the real commander was Colonel Thomas Kelly. Although American aid would still be solicited, the effective base for Fenian operations would be among the Irish immigrants in Britain, since Kelly had established an Irish provisional government in Manchester.[38] Lacking Stephens's prestige, Kelly was unable to take over complete control for he could not prevent McCafferty from establishing an independent Irish Directorate in London.[39]

The movement now lacked political leadership and was in the hands of military men who would spur one another into action by mutual accusations of cowardice and treason. While the movement's leaders still planned an uprising by an underground militia, they could not prevent isolated acts of terrorism and local risings which were not part of an accepted general plan. Stephens had forbidden the assassination of informers, and by 1867 so many informers appeared among the Fenian leaders that assassination could not be prevented.

The British government was kept informed of all important plans made by Kelly and McCafferty by two key informers, John Joseph Corydon and Godfrey Massey. Corydon, who had gained O'Mahony's confidence, was employed as a messenger between Fenian leaders in Britain. When Fenian leaders moved to the Midlands, Corydon established connections with Head Constable Richard McHale of the Irish constabulary, stationed in Liverpool to monitor Fenian activities.[40] Godfrey Massey had served as a non-commissioned officer in the Crimean War and had become a colonel in the Confederate forces. He was employed as a commercial traveller when he joined the Fenian organization after the Civil War. His former military rank probably ensured his acceptance into the inner circles of the Fenians and he was present when Stephens was deposed in December 1866. Massey had established contact with Consul Archibald by the time that he was given the rank of brigadier general by Kelly and sent to the Midlands as part of the Fenian High Command.[41]

The new phase of Fenianism was personified by John McCafferty, the former Confederate officer who had served with Morgan's raiders. He had threatened to kill Stephens in December and after the demise of Fenianism was to become involved in the purely terrorist "Invincibles".[42] McCafferty had conceived a desperate plan to seize Chester Castle on February 11, 1867, a plan he confided to Corydon after it had been rejected by Kelly. By this project, McCafferty hoped to seize the ten thousand stand of arms kept in the castle and place them on board a train heading for Holyhead, where he would then commandeer a number of boats and sail for Ireland.[43]

The first stage of the plan had some chance of success as the castle was guarded by only a handful of men, and over one thousand Fenians arrived at Chester by train on the appointed day. As Corydon had alerted authorities, the Fenians found the castle well-guarded and reinforcements arriving by train. Most of them prudently returned to their homes, but about sixty, including McCafferty himself, decided to proceed to Ireland where they were put under arrest.[44]

The rising that took place in Ireland on March 5, 1867 would never have been authorized by Stephens. General Cluseret refused to take command on the grounds that the ten thousand men he required could not be provided. The plan of the rising was to disrupt communications and wage a guerrilla campaign in the hope that the revolt would be supported by British radicals or perhaps inspire a series of revolutions on the scale of 1848. Cluseret was already convinced that there would be no help from Britain and that European revolutionaries who found London a convenient base of operations would not risk offending the British government for the sake of Ireland.

It is difficult to say how much faith Kelly had in his plans for the uprising, but he sensed the need for some kind of a military demonstration if Fenian forces were not to disintegrate without striking a blow. In making this decision, he gave the Irish Fenians a place in history at the cost of disrupting what remained of their organization. As in 1848, the uprising was little more than a series of incidents. Several thousand Fenians assembled outside Dublin and seized two police barracks, but dispersed before the arrival of troops. Similar action was carried out by smaller numbers around Cork, and Fenian bands gathered in Tipperary, Limerick, Clare, Queen's County, and Louth.[45] Very few of those turning out could be armed or placed under the command of trained officers. By March 9, flying columns of military and police were hunting out surviving bands of Fenians and preparations were underway for another series of political trials. The case against the Fenians would be strong because the principal informers, Corydon and Massey, were to appear as witnesses for the Crown.[46]

Colonel Kelly fled to England where he established his headquarters at Manchester. Roberts arrived in Paris, hoping to take over the leadership of the Irish Fenians, but his efforts were defeated by a convention which Kelly held secretly in midsummer in Manchester. Here plans were made for the establishment of a new institution in America, the Clan-na-Gael. Membership was to be by invitation, as in the case of the Ancient Order of Hibernians and the Hunters Lodges, one of the first indications that the Fenians were adopting the classic form of a secret society and giving up the pretence that they represented a mass movement preparing for imminent revolution.[47] Henceforth, there would be no grand strategy of revolution in the style of O'Mahony and Stephens, but more independent activity by the various fragments of the movement, interspersed with isolated acts of terrorism.

Kelly was arrested September 11, 1867 and released by the daring action of his followers who killed a policeman in the course of the rescue. Five of those engaged in the rescue were arrested and condemned to death. The three who were hanged on November 23, 1867 — Allen, Larkin, and O'Brien — were henceforth known as the "Manchester Martyrs".[48] The killing of an English policeman on English soil made it difficult for authorities to follow the established formula of commuting the death sentences. The result was that the clergy, Constitutionalists, and Fenians were brought together in protest against the executions, as tens of thousands paraded in Dublin in a manner reminiscent of the MacManus funeral.[49]

After his rescue, Kelly returned to America, but the arrest of Ricard O'Sullivan Burke, who had been involved in freeing Kelly, led to a second and more serious incident. Burke attempted to organize his own escape by authorizing his followers to place a quantity of gunpowder against the wall of Clerkenwell prison where he was held. Blowing up the wall while the prisoners were being exercised was supposed to provide Burke with an opportunity to escape. As the authorities had been warned, Burke was not in the yard when the explosion took place, but the explosion destroyed tenements outside the prison, killing 12 people and injuring 120 others.[50]

As Kelly was presumed to be responsible for the explosion, its authors were denounced by the Roberts wing of Fenianism. Yet more serious was the reaction of public opinion in England, which the authorities feared would lead to attacks on the Irish in England.[51] The Clerkenwell explosion was typical of the new phase of Fenianism which was also marked by a robbery of a gunshop in Ireland on November 28 and a rather pointless raid on a martello tower in County Cork. A more successful raid on a powder magazine was carried out early in the new year. This incident appears to have been under the direction of William Mackey Lomasney, usually referred to as Captain Mackey, whom Kelly had appointed his successor. Lomasney apparently had no higher purpose than keeping the Fenians busy and his resistance to arrest on February 7, during which another policeman was killed, was perhaps intended as an example for others to follow.[52]

Moreover, early in 1868, the Dublin Metropolitan Police arrested what appeared to be an assassination committee which had evidently been in existence since the end of 1865.[53] This was probably an informal body operating without the knowledge of Stephens. With the appearance of Massey and Corydon as Crown witnesses, it was evident that informers posed a serious threat to the movement and, whatever policy Fenian leaders adopted, informers were likely to suffer at the hands of Fenian sympathizers.

## THE FENIANS AT SEA

American Fenians, however, while they remained on American soil, had little to fear from informers, and taking measures against them would involve collision with American authorities. Furthermore, the quarrels of American Fenians and their tendency to expose one another's projects made it difficult for informers in the American movement to get beyond information already provided by the Fenian press. Indeed, informers, British agents, and McMicken's detectives had such difficulty in distinguishing between Fenian projects and serious plans that their reports induced the Canadian government to take expensive precautions against imaginary dangers.[54]

The American Fenians were not only less endangered by spies and informers, but in 1867 they remained under political, not military, leaders. The Roberts wing held picnics and parades in cities along the frontier, accompanied by threats of imminent invasion. Yet their treasury was empty and it was too soon to try the patience of American border authorities a second time. The O'Mahony wing was led by Gleeson who became actual leader after Kelly had left for Ireland. In order to

raise money for Kelly's departure for Ireland, Gleeson had
found it necessary to sell two thousand stand of arms at re-
duced rates.[55] Many American Fenians were travelling to Ireland at their own expense, and whatever doubts existed concerning the fortunes of the Irish movement, they were dispelled
by news of the rising in Ireland.[56] Its insignificance and failure
made no difference, as defeat could be interpreted as a preliminary skirmish to a general rising.

Gleeson launched a series of public meetings, negotiations
were opened with the Roberts wing, and telegrams sent to John
Mitchel offering him the leadership of the combined American movement. Mitchel refused at once on the grounds that
success was impossible while England was at peace, and he
made it clear that he did not approve of raising money to aid
a supposed rebellion. As a result of Mitchel's refusal, a convention was hurriedly arranged in New York. Anthony B.
Griffin replaced Gleeson as chief of the former O'Mahony
wing, while Roberts held a convention in Utica, New York,
to discuss further plans for invading Canada.[57]

This evidence of Fenian revival started a new series of gestures towards the Irish electorate, beginning with a speech
from the Democratic leader in New York, Fernando Woods,
who argued that Americans should promote republicanism in
Europe because Europeans were introducing monarchy in
America, citing Maximilian's Mexico and the forthcoming
Canadian Confederation. Ignatius Donnelly, author of a
widely read book on Atlantis, demanded belligerent rights for
the "Irish People" while Nathaniel Banks,[58] congressional representative for Massachusetts and a former Know-Nothing
candidate, asked for American intervention on behalf of
Fenians held in Canada. Gleeson himself was invited to lec-
ture the House Committee on Foreign Affairs on the historical
background of British tyranny in Ireland.[59]

While politicians were offering this moral support for the
Irish rising, Roberts sought to organize military support by
renewing efforts against Canada. He had no forces prepared to
act at this time. Yet the threat of invasion announced in a
series of state conventions held in places as far apart as Maine

and California might prove useful if they could induce Britain to move troops to Canada or provoke the Canadian government into calling out the militia.

The responsibility for providing direct support rested with Gleeson, since he was titular head of the forces which Kelly was organizing in Ireland. In response to Kelly's appeals for aid, the Fenians acquired in early April the *Jacmel Packet,* a vessel of 138 tons.[60] The *Jacmel* was loaded with five thousand stand of arms, several small field pieces, and a plentiful supply of ammunition. Rechristened *Erin's Hope,* the packet sailed for Ireland on April 13, 1867 and arrived off Sligo Bay on May 23, carrying thirty-eight Fenians, including one who was to turn informer. They made contact with the Fenian leader, Ricard O'Sullivan Burke, who advised them against an attack on the town of Sligo as the uprising was over. On June 1, thirty-one were landed near Dungarvon Bay. Of these, twenty-eight were arrested within twenty-four hours, adding substantially to the number of Fenians to be tried in Dublin. The *Jacmel* then returned to New York without landing its munitions in Ireland.[61]

Throughout this episode, the Roberts wing had continued its threats against Canada. These were taken seriously, not only by the Canadian government, but also by General George Meade who was sent again to the frontier by the United States government. What various observers of Fenianism at this time appear to have neglected was the weakness of Fenian financial resources, which had been relatively strong in 1866.[62] So far was Roberts from making serious plans for invading Canada that he had, as noted previously, left for Paris in the summer of 1867 in an effort to take over the leadership of the Fenian movement in Ireland and Britain.

Up to this time, the inner councils of the Roberts wing had been free from informers, but in June, while Roberts was in Paris, Rudolph Fitzpatrick, Roberts's Assistant Secretary of War, made contact with the acting British consul in New York.[63] A year later, Thomas Beach, alias Henri Le Caron, who had already written reports on the Fenians for the Foreign Office, joined the Roberts wing and, by gaining the confidence of General John O'Neill, was able to keep British and Canadian authorities aware of designs against Canada.[64]

## THE ASSASSINATION OF MCGEE

With Confederation accomplished in 1867, there was no place in the new federal cabinet for D'Arcy McGee as John A. Macdonald found it more convenient to draw the representative of the Irish Catholic community from the Maritimes. At the same time George Brown, who was again in the opposition, was courting the Catholic vote by nominating Catholic candidates to run in the election to the new federal parliament.[65] McGee accepted the necessity of his exclusion from the cabinet, and he prepared to run in his old constituency in Montreal West and, as well, to contest the seat of Prescott as candidate for the new Ontario provincial assembly. Pluralism of this kind was acceptable at the time, and by running in Prescott where there were nine hundred Catholics out of a total of 2,100 voters, McGee might make the point that his influence extended beyond Montreal.[66]

At first it did not seem that the Fenians would become involved in the first Canadian federal election. With the departure of Michael Murphy from Toronto, the Hibernians, now led by Patrick Boyle, lost much of their belligerence. They had planned to parade to Mass with brass bands and insignia on St. Patrick's Day, 1867,[67] but abandoned their plans when the bishop indicated his disapproval. D'Arcy McGee was still being denounced by them as an informer and compared to Corydon and Massey,[68] but they had previously compared him to Goulah Sullivan. Yet Boyle, in the *Irish Canadian*, also denounced the authors of the Clerkenwell explosion, insisting that it could not have been the work of Fenians, an indication that Boyle himself was not fully aware of the changing character of the Fenian movement.

Moreover, Boyle's support of the "Catholic convention", called at Kingston to secure Catholic votes for George Brown, revealed his inclination to return to conventional politics.[69]

To do this he would have to retain his influence over the votes of Fenian sympathizers. Nonetheless, if Fenian votes were to be used effectively, they would have to be used quietly lest they prove an embarrassment to those receiving them.

In Montreal, where Fenians were able to find allies among the personal and political enemies of McGee, it was very different. This informal coalition against McGee, first noticeable in 1861 at the time of the *Trent* affair, had irritated McGee on several occasions. The Montreal Fenians made the initial mistake of creating a local Hibernian Club which attracted few members and advertised its Fenian sympathies. By 1865, this effort was virtually abandoned and the Fenians were able to infiltrate the loyalist St. Patrick's Society of Montreal,[70] and fully exploit the unpopularity McGee had acquired as a result of his Wexford speech. Yet the Montreal Fenian sympathizers would not have been able to assert themselves had it not been for the opportunity presented by the election of 1867, and the apparent acquiescence of McGee's political rival, Bernard Devlin, in Fenian attacks upon McGee.[71]

There were three wards in McGee's constituency of Montreal West — St. Antoine which was largely Protestant, St. Lawrence which was French Canadian, and Ste. Anne's which was the Irish area. Devlin could not hope to win the Protestant vote and had a limited appeal to French Canadians. It was consequently essential for him to destroy McGee's character among the Irish.

There had been a long tradition of electoral violence among the Irish of Montreal, beginning with the election of Daniel Tracey in 1832.[72] The Irish had rioted in favour of loyalist candidates in the election of 1841, and had been organized by Francis Hincks to support Reformers in 1844. Again in 1848 and 1853, Irish elements were involved in serious Montreal disorders and riots.[73] In 1867 there seemed to have been a disposition among a substantial section of the Irish in Ste. Anne's ward to follow the lead of those who offered opportunities for violence. The campaign which the Fenians had been waging against McGee offered an acceptable pretext, particularly as it could be combined with support of a respectable political candidate.

At the opening of the election campaign, McGee wrote to John A. Macdonald that he had decided not to go to Toronto as it would provide the "Grit Fenians" with an opportunity to offer him insults. In his initial speech in Montreal, McGee stressed his attachment to the interests of the entire Dominion, describing George Brown and Joseph Howe as representatives of sectional interests.[74] Bernard Devlin had begun his campaign a few days earlier by emphasizing his desire to represent all shades of Irish opinion, presumably placing the Fenians within the range of his sympathies.

At first, McGee was more worried about his campaign in Prescott, for John A. Macdonald had agreed to support an Ontario coalition headed by Sandfield Macdonald, the liberal leader who was supporting McGee's opponent in Prescott. While McGee was busy in Prescott, Devlin launched a personal attack on him, recalling McGee's former rebel connections. He declared that McGee was needlessly provoking the Fenians by denouncing them, and he again condemned McGee for his Wexford speech. As McGee was not at the moment making much of the Fenians, it was Devlin who was anxious to bring the issue into the current campaign.[75]

Meanwhile, the bishops of Ontario either supported the coalition government of John A. Macdonald or, like Bishop Lynch of Toronto, adopted an attitude of benevolent neutrality. In Quebec, four bishops announced their acceptance of Confederation, which was useful to the Macdonald–Cartier government. McGee received moral support from Archbishop Connolly of Halifax in the form of a letter to the Montreal *Gazette* published on August 1, but he did not enjoy the support of Bishop Ignace Bourget of Montreal, or his paper, the *True Witness*.[76]

If it had been merely a matter of newspaper controversy and debate, McGee could have overwhelmed his opponents without undue reference to the Fenians. The only hope of McGee's enemies was to prevent him from speaking in public and this they set out to do. When McGee tried to hold a series of three meetings early in August in each of the Montreal wards, he managed to speak in the face of considerable opposition at the first meeting, but was assaulted by an egg-throwing crowd at the second, and managed to speak only with the aid of police protection at the third in Point St. Charles. As McGee had received threats through the mail, he had no doubt about the source of this opposition. He decided to accept the challenge and to make Fenianism the issue of the election.[77]

McGee declared that he had strangled Fenianism and would not be annoyed by its carcase. He promised that he would publish the full facts about Fenianism in the press, based on documents which he had had in his possession for two years. McGee also stated that he had been told that if he left the Fenians alone, they would leave him alone.[78] It seems unlikely that McGee could have bought peace with silence, because it was Devlin, not McGee, who had introduced Fenianism into the election campaign. The Fenians were in need of a visible and vulnerable enemy against whom they could direct their indignation, and attacking McGee gave them a part to play in electoral politics.

Two weeks later, while McGee was walking to his committee rooms in Griffintown, he was pelted with stones, and soon found that it was virtually impossible to hold a public meeting in Montreal. He then left for Prescott, arranging to have his exposé of Fenianism published in his absence.[79] In this series of articles, McGee traced the origins of Fenianism to the *Trent* affair, explaining that the Fenians had been responsible for the refusal of a number of railway police to take the loyalty oath during the Fenian invasions of 1866. He also asserted that Fenians had gained influence in the St. Patrick's Society of Montreal, of which Devlin was president.

In the course of exposing Fenian influence, McGee implied much more than he could prove, particularly in regard to Devlin's connection with the Fenians. But Devlin seemed content to ignore the violence against McGee, while McGee's attacks on the Fenians stimulated further verbal attacks upon himself from as far afield as Quebec City and Toronto.

On August 29, nomination day, McGee again found himself unable to speak. As voting was still by open ballot, the kind of intimidation that mobs could exert might frighten his supporters away from the polls. McGee complained that his friends were receiving threats that their homes and places of business would be burned if they gave him their votes.[80] In spite of this and the news of McGee's defeat at Prescott, which reached Montreal the day before the election there, McGee won by a slight majority in Montreal West but he ran behind Devlin in the Irish Ste. Anne's ward.

When McGee's victory was announced, Devlin's supporters attacked McGee's committee rooms at the Mechanics Institute, apparently under the impression that he was inside.[81] McGee may well have reflected at the time that it was but a little over ten years since his life had been endangered by Toronto Orangemen. Being attacked by Orangemen in 1857 had increased his prestige among the Irish. Attacks by Fenians in the year of Confederation would increase his stature among loyalists, but Fenians at this time were more formidable enemies than the Orangemen, and McGee's attacks on their influence in the St. Patrick's Society ensured that the feud with Devlin and the Fenians would survive the election.

There was undoubtedly some fear among Fenian sympathizers in Montreal that they might suffer from McGee's exposé, but this seems to have been less important than the feeling that they had been out-manoeuvred and ridiculed by an unscrupulous and clever man. The state of feelings a month after the election is indicated by an encounter between McGee and Devlin, described in George E. Clerk's diary: "Oct. 2, Wednesday — a row between Devlin and McGee . . . Devlin spat in McGee's face near Post Office."[82]

Evidence of hostility towards McGee within the St. Patrick's Society had appeared shortly after Devlin became president in April 1865, just a month before McGee's Wexford speech. McGee attributed this to Fenian influence, declaring that the society's executive had been corresponding with O'Mahony and that the evidence of this correspondence had been destroyed by a convenient fire on January 14, 1867.[83] A week later, the society's chaplain, Father Patrick Dowd, warned against internal dissensions, but there were no further developments until the election.[84]

In October, the executive decided to expel McGee from the society and gave notice to that effect. McGee responded by telling the House of Commons that suspension of habeas corpus should remain in force because there was evidence of Fenian influence in the St. Patrick's Society of Montreal. The St. Patrick's Society, in a resolution, condemned McGee for calumny against the society, but made no further effort to expel him.

McGee responded with further charges, declaring that O'Mahony had addressed a meeting attended by Bernard Devlin, his brother, Owen Devlin, and others who had become prominent in the St. Patrick's Society, such as F. B. MacNamee who had collected money for the American Fenians.[85] Yet moves to turn out McGee were delayed until the opening of the new year when he was formally expelled. Bernard Devlin was not present at this meeting and there was only one dissenting vote against McGee's expulsion. The reasons given were McGee's charges against the society. It was declared that the books of the society, including the minutes, had been inspected and signed by a number of public persons, including the mayor of Montreal.[86] McGee's friend and supporter, Brown Chamberlin, editor of the *Gazette,* published a list of the sixty members who had attended the meeting, making it evident that the gathering was dominated by those who had worked for Devlin in the last election.

McGee's health had suffered considerably in the course of the election and, as he was heavily in debt, he was prepared to abandon politics for a civil service appointment and to devote more time to his literary career. Although a man of his talents could hardly retire permanently from politics, his political fortunes were in eclipse and posed a threat to no one. Yet the campaign against McGee by the Fenians continued. Threatening letters arrived from Ireland, the United States, and Montreal.[87]

The Fenians had always asserted themselves more by threats than by action, and the seriousness with which such threats were treated was a measure of Fenian influence. In 1868, it was almost impossible to make a balanced estimate of the danger of renewed raids across the frontier or for McGee and his friends to judge the degree to which his life was in danger. In retrospect, it does not appear that the plans for immediate renewal of raids across the frontier were taken seriously by most of those who made them, nor does it seem that there was a concerted plan to assassinate McGee.

His assassination on April 7, 1868 had the character of an accident in that it was the work of men who usually failed in their attempts. Patrick James Whelan, who was convicted and executed for the assassination, belonged to the general class which found Fenianism most attractive. He was apprenticed as a tailor at the age of fourteen, and had acquired a competence in the trade. For nine years he had served in the British army, three of them in India, and he came to Canada in 1865.[88] Like Michael Murphy, Whelan belonged to the tradition of the Ribbonmen rather than to the more intellectual tradition of the Irish republicans. It is impossible to say whether he had even become a formal member of the Fenian Brotherhood. His brother, Joseph Whelan, had been among those exiled from Ireland for his part in the 1867 rising. Yet James Whelan was unquestionably under the influence of Fenian propaganda and had been engaged in some kind of clandestine work on their behalf.

His frequent changes of employment even when his conditions of work had been satisfactory, and his employment as regimental tailor in Toronto, Kingston, and Quebec City, all garrison towns, suggest that he may have been carrying on propaganda among Irish soldiers in the army. In Quebec City he was arrested as a Fenian but the charges against him were dropped. During the election campaign of 1867, he had worked as a scrutineer for Devlin[89] and at the time of his arrest on the charge of assassinating McGee, he had in his possession a badge of the Toronto Hibernian Society and a copy of the Fenian New York *Irish American*.

During his trial, Whelan insisted that he was not a Fenian and that he was innocent of McGee's assassination. There were no creditable witnesses to the actual shooting of McGee. In spite of this the evidence against Whelan was very strong. His presence in Prescott during McGee's campaign there, his return to Montreal when McGee returned, and his taking up employment in Ottawa when McGee took his seat in parliament[90] all suggest that he was stalking McGee.

In 1866 Whelan had married a fairly prosperous Montreal boarding-house keeper, slightly older than himself, and his employment in Ottawa involved separation from his wife. During the election excitement he had announced before a variety of witnesses, both friends and enemies, his intention of killing McGee, but those who heard the threats do not appear to have taken them too seriously.[91]

On January 1, 1868, Whelan and a friend, Michael Enright, had gone to McGee's house at two o'clock in the morning. They awakened McGee's family and only Whelan was admitted into the house, the door being locked behind him by McGee's brother. Whelan gave his name as Smith and warned McGee that an attempt would be made to burn his house at four o'clock that morning. McGee thanked Whelan for the warning and gave him a note to take to the police station which Whelan did not deliver until nearly five o'clock.[92] This visit could have been either an attempted assassination, a reconnaissance, or merely an effort to harass McGee.

Whelan had acquired a revolver some time in 1866 which was of the same calibre as that which killed McGee. He had been in and out of the parliamentary gallery, watching McGee the night of the assassination, and had left the House shortly after McGee, nor had he any witness to support his statement that he went directly home.

After the trial, on the eve of his execution, Whelan signed a statement that he was present at the assassination but had not fired the shot.[93] This statement is consistent with recent opinion of ballistic experts that the bullet which killed McGee, although it could have been fired from Whelan's gun, could not have come from a box of cartridges of the kind that Whelan was carrying.[94] Moreover, evidence of assassination committees in Ireland indicated that two men were normally employed when assassination was involved, and Whelan had been accompanied by Michael Enright during his visit to McGee's home on January 1, 1868.

Although the *Irish Canadian* was concerned about prejudice against Whelan and some of the evidence presented by the prosecution, its editor was satisfied that justice was done on the grounds that since Whelan had admitted his presence at the murder, he was guilty as an accessory to the fact.[95] As Whelan's statement had not been made at the trial, the jury condemned him on circumstantial evidence. His defence counsel, Orange Grand Master John Hillyard Cameron, stated that the circumstantial evidence was consistent with both guilt and innocence, while during the course of the trial the defence had raised serious doubts about the credibility of the evidence given by Crown witnesses whose testimony linked Whelan directly to the crime.

Whelan's statement that he knew who killed D'Arcy McGee lent authority to his insistence that the others arrested and accused had no part in the murder. It is possible that he acted alone and wished to help his friends without contradicting his statement that he had not killed McGee. If this supposition is dismissed, then the presence of two at the assassination lends some credibility to the case for conspiracy which was supported by the testimony of some of the Crown witnesses, but certainly not proved at the trial.

This version suggests that a group of Fenian sympathizers in Montreal discussed the matter of killing McGee over the Christmas holidays. The visit to McGee's home on January 1 was an effort that failed. It is certainly true that a number of Whelan's friends who became waiters at the Russell Hotel in Ottawa had left Montreal about the same time as Whelan had. It is difficult to go much beyond this and, if it were not for the evidence of the bullet, it would be easier to believe that Whelan had been making threats to kill McGee which were not taken seriously by his friends, and that, after stalking McGee on several occasions, he finally found an opportunity to carry out his threats.

Evidence that Fenians were turning towards terrorism at this time can be found not only in incidents already related, but also in the attack on Prince Alfred, the Duke of Edinburgh, in Australia, the killing of an informer by the son of Michael Doheny, and the wounding of Patrick Meehan[96] in a dispute among leaders of the Roberts wing. McCafferty, who was released from prison in 1871, demonstrated his addiction to terrorism by his participation in the Phoenix Park murders in 1885 in which several persons were killed in efforts to assassinate the viceroy of Ireland.[97]

There is, however, no evidence connecting the assassination with the American Fenians, who disliked McGee but could hardly share the feelings of Whelan and his friends. So closely were American Fenians monitored by various informers and McMicken's frontier detectives, that it is inconceivable that an assassination plot could have escaped their notice.

Although Patrick Boyle of the *Irish Canadian* protested that Fenians were presumed guilty of McGee's assassination without evidence, he expressed his horror at the deed. A few days later he reported the death, from natural causes, of Michael Murphy in Buffalo, Murphy being the man who had been the personification of everything McGee opposed in Irish Canadian politics.[98] In Montreal, McGee's funeral became, in effect, an anti-Fenian demonstration led by the Irish Canadian community.[99]

In the excitement that followed the assassination, Boyle was arrested and held for five months while the *Irish Canadian* suspended publication until his release early in August 1868. Although Boyle renounced none of his Fenian sympathies, there was a noticeable change in the policy of the *Irish Canadian* after his release. Under the heading "Give Ireland what Canada Has", he found Canadian institutions to be superior to American, and praised the system that had just imprisoned him for five months. He also made a point of praising George Brown for the moral support that the *Globe* had offered during his period of arrest.[100]

Even more significant was the absence of comment on the futility of legal action in Ireland and Boyle's interest in returning independent candidates in the coming elections in the United Kingdom. Boyle had apparently returned to O'Connellite politics, but could not openly abandon Fenians without alienating his readers. He offered cautious sympathy for Whelan, but there was surprisingly little done for the accused by Fenian sympathizers during his trial.

Efforts were made to organize a picnic to raise money for the prisoners accused of complicity in McGee's assassination, but

Bernard Devlin denounced these efforts as dangerous to the good name and reputation of the Irish Canadian community. Boyle printed Devlin's letter, but expressed the view that Whelan's friends had a right to raise money on his behalf.[101] Boyle was prepared to offer sympathy to Fenians when it was needed, but the Toronto Hibernians evidently had no inclination to co-ordinate their activities with the various factions of the Fenian movement. The most obvious sign of this was their accommodation with Bishop Lynch, who accepted their acclamation from the balcony of his palace on St. Patrick's Day 1869.[102] The following year there would be a formal condemnation of Fenianism by the Vatican and a second Fenian attempt against Canada. There was still a network of Fenian circles in Canada, sustained by the anticipation of coming invasion, but it was no longer possible for them to control an organized body of sympathizers.

## THE 1870 INVASION

In America, the efforts made in 1867 to unite all factions of the movement under John Mitchel failed because Mitchel refused the leadership, at first politely. But Mitchel's intense dislike of Stephens and his movement induced him to write a more devastating condemnation of Fenianism than McGee had made in his Wexford speech. This was in the form of a letter, obviously intended for publication, which he sent to the Irish Constitutionalist, John Martin.[103] In his letter, Mitchel declared that Fenianism was established on a "false basis by that wretched Stephens, upon the prospect of immediate insurrection in Ireland, while England is at peace . . . aided by forces and arms from this country, contrary to the laws of the United States."

Mitchel went on to say: "Our people are credulous, enthusiastic, impatient . . . a tempting material for a charlatan . . . . The people in Ireland have been deluded by false representations of the power and resources of the Irish American nation here, and the Irish Americans have been grossly deceived as to the power and resources of the revolutionary element in Ireland."

Mitchel admitted that the Fenians had a formidable force of trained men under their command in America "but it is on one side of the Atlantic and its objective is on the other". With regard to the Fenian attempts against Canada, he said, "It looks easier to carry armed forces across that frontier than across the Atlantic . . . yet it is impossible . . . to bring over any force at all adequate to the service." Mitchel compared the Fenians to a bulldog kept on a leash by the American government which could relax its grip occasionally to frighten the British.

In spite of this, General John O'Neill proceeded with plans for a final attack on Canada. The former O'Mahony wing came under the leadership of a literary man, John Savage. Savage made little effort to become a conspirator, so O'Neill went ahead with a series of plans reminiscent of 1866, although his real object was to gain a second victory on the scale of Ridgeway. Yet the conditions which had made Ridgeway possible no longer existed. The Canadian militia was better organized and trained. McMicken's detectives had become more efficient and the American authorities, under the recently elected Grant administration, were less concerned about the Irish vote.

O'Neill's one chance was the rapid mobilization of a relatively small force at a point near the frontier where the local defence was weak. This was virtually excluded by the publicity surrounding a quarrel which broke out between O'Neill and his own senate and in the presence of his adjutant, Henri Le Caron, who was a British agent in continuous contact with the Canadian government.[104]

Le Caron had written an extensive report on January 21, 1870, explaining to McMicken in detail O'Neill's invasion plans.[105] O'Neill hoped to put nine hundred cavalry and 2,400 infantry across the frontier within twenty-four hours. It was suggested that Le Caron, because of his command of French, be sent westward to contact Louis Riel, but O'Neill declared that Le Caron was indispensable in the east.

Le Caron's special task was to collect arms and munitions for the coming invasion, and it was therefore possible for the Canadian government to inform American authorities where

the Fenian arms depots were located. Governor Henry Hoff-
man of New York, mindful of the Irish vote, promised the
Fenians that he would delay as much as possible complying
with any request from the United States federal government
for co-operation and support.[106]

McMicken met Le Caron near the border on February 12,
1870 and was told to expect the raid sometime towards the
end of March and that Fenians in Montreal had promised to
cut the telegraph and railway lines.[107] There is much information concerning Fenian plans in Montreal and it is likely that
Montreal Fenians had a tenuous contact with O'Neill, but
there is no reason to believe that there was an organized movement in Montreal willing and able to act.[108]

As O'Neill was unable to keep to his original time-table, he
had to face his congress and the revolt of his senators. In the
ensuing quarrel, the senate leader, Patrick Meehan, was shot
but not killed.[109] The followers of O'Neill and his enemies
met in separate conventions called in Chicago and New York.
O'Neill set the date of the raid into Canada for the 24th of
May—the Queen's birthday. The American cabinet decided
not to seize Fenian arms collected for what might remain a
mere project, but rather to act promptly once the Fenians
moved across the frontier. Canadian authorities, being informed of Fenian intentions to attack on May 24, kept the
troops gathered to celebrate the Queen's birthday under arms
in Montreal in spite of rain. At four o'clock in the afternoon
they were told of the expected raid and entrained for the
frontier.[110]

In spite of rumours of the movement of several thousand
Fenians along the frontier, O'Neill had only a few hundred
under his command in Franklin, Vermont, on the 24th of
May. At noon the following day, he marched two hundred
men across the frontier and fell back with two casualties, one
killed and one wounded, after an exchange of volleys with
seventy-five loyalist volunteers. When his men refused to move
forward, he re-crossed the frontier to get reinforcements, but
was arrested by Thomas Forster, a United States marshal.[111]

The next day a force of Fenians crossed the frontier near
Malone, New York, but it retired after having a man killed.

There were no Canadian casualties in either engagement. President Ulysses Grant promptly issued a proclamation denouncing the invasion on the day of the raid. The previous president had waited five days before similar action.[112]

The Canadian public had not taken the rumours of a coming raid seriously, and the opposition press had expressed irritation at the preparation and calling out of troops, measures which rebounded in favour of the administration when the raids took place. The vague plans of the Fenians for a liaison with Louis Riel remained a project with no chance of success.

The long-standing question of the status of British subjects who had become American citizens, which had caused difficulties during the times of the Hunters Lodges and the Fenian raids, was settled by the naturalization treaty, signed on May 13, 1870 on the eve of the last Fenian raid. After 1870 the Fenians survived as an "old boys'" association, the exception being those organized in the relatively small Clan-na-Gael.

The decline of the Fenians is indicated by the attempt to bring them into a new confederation of Irish American societies. This appeal was made by five Irish exiles who arrived in New York on the Cunard liner, *Cuba*, on January 19, 1871. Hailed as the "Cuba Five",[113] the exiles were courted by Republicans and Democrats interested in the Irish vote. General O'Neill joined the confederation, but was expelled when he crossed the Canadian frontier the third time in 1871 and seized Pembina, Manitoba. Instead of rallying to O'Neill, Louis Riel, at the request of the lieutenant governor, paraded three hundred volunteers, all prepared to march against the invaders.[114] O'Neill was arrested and released again by American authorities. This small excursion caused some alarm in Manitoba, but did not seriously disturb the Canadian government.

Patrick Boyle continued to edit the *Irish Canadian,* but his support of Irish nationalism did not prevent John A. Macdonald from making efforts to bring him into the conservative orbit. Macdonald's efforts did not succeed but his thoughts on the subject provide a kind of epitaph on Canadian Fenianism. He wrote:

The paper [the *Irish Canadian*] might be as factious as it pleased about Irish home politics, or even New York movements, for all I could care, as long as it pursued a course that would keep up its present subscription list and influence. With respect to Canadian politics, it should not suddenly veer round, as that would excite suspicion, but it should cease to advocate the junction of Grits and Catholics and by degrees after the next election come round to support Ministerial candidates. It could easily do so on the ground that it sees that fairness is at last being done to Irishmen.

# CHAPTER SIX

# Conclusions

Although Irish immigrants to America readily accepted the institutions of their adopted country, their sense of nationality, based on history, ancestry, tradition, and religion, did not blend easily with "Americanism". This historic conception of nationality, strengthened by the efforts of Irish intellectuals under the influence of the Romantic movement, posed a challenge to the American idea of nationality formed under the influence of the Enlightenment and based on geography and political theory.

In Canada, Irish nationalism at first caused little tension because the preservation of trans-Atlantic traditions was consistent with being subjects of an oceanic empire. Irish nationalists might be denounced as disloyal, but it was difficult to abuse them as foreigners because nativism was contrary to the loyalist tradition and could be condemned as treason. Orangemen might continue their quarrel with Catholics, but they were also immigrants, and Catholicism was part of the Canadian landscape not only in French Canada but in areas where Scottish Catholics were the original settlers.

The Irish Catholics who came to the fiercely Protestant eighteenth-century America did not escape from religious intolerance, and it is not surprising that many were found serving with the loyalists in Boston and New York during the

American Revolution. In Ireland there was articulate sympathy for the American cause among Protestant nationalists, but the Catholic Committee found it expedient to raise volunteers for the Crown forces serving in America. It was not until the organization of the United Irish Society during the French Revolution that Irish Catholics on both sides of the Atlantic became active nationalists and republicans.

The founding of United Irish Societies in the United States marked the first efforts to create a trans-Atlantic political movement linking American republicanism to the cause of international revolution. It would be impossible to create a similar organization in Canada because the United Irish Society was an illegal organization and its agents, if discovered, could be arrested. The United Irishmen and other supporters of "Jacobin principles" enjoyed sympathy among Jeffersonian Democrats, but were not welcomed by the governing Federalist party. As the Catholic church was opposed to the French Revolution, there was no connection between anti-Papist and anti-Jacobin sentiment until the United Irish attempted to use a Catholic church as a base for agitation against the Federalist-inspired Alien and Sedition Act.

Irish republicanism became a powerful force in Ireland during the last decade of the century, but it did not long survive the rebellion of 1798. It lingered on until the end of the Napoleonic wars, sustained by the hopes of United Irish exiles in France and America. In America, these hopes reached a climax during the war of 1812 when the Irish again aroused the antipathy of the Federalists by their enthusiasm for an unpopular war.

With the end of the war, the United Irish exiles were assimilated into American society and the new waves of immigrants and their priests, who arrived with them, were under the influence of Daniel O'Connell. As the champion of equal rights for Catholics and of independence for Ireland, O'Connell might appeal to American principles but, being a monarchist, he could not appeal to them as a fellow republican. Any disadvantage that arose from this would have been balanced by the fact that his followers would not, like the United Irishmen, create problems in Anglo-American relations by making the United States a base for conspiracies.

Neither O'Connell and the Irish clergy, nor, until 1848, the younger generation of Romantic nationalists like Duffy and McGee, believed that republicanism was suited to the needs of Irish nationalism. Although the American republic was, at times, praised as an established institution, international republicanism was revolutionary and anti-clerical. It demanded illegal activity and association with Mazzini and others who were organizing conspiracies in the Papal States. Republican agitation would alienate the Irish hierarchy and make it impossible to secure the support of the clergy who were prepared to encourage constitutional agitation. Moreover, there was the danger that preparations for a rising would re-animate the alliance between the Irish government and the Orangemen, an alliance which O'Connell had painstakingly helped to dissolve during the 1820s.

The peasantry would use violence to redress local grievances, but they had no interest in the republican idea and were reluctant to accept the discipline involved in preparations for a general rising. Neither the American nor the French republicans of 1848 would support a republican crusade in Ireland and even Mazzini was reluctant to offend the British government for the sake of the Irish who raised volunteers to defend the Papal States.

While O'Connell's influence prevailed, the Irish Americans would make no effort to organize an Irish republican movement which might prove an embarrassment to Irish nationalists in the British provinces. Yet they emphasized their attachment to republican institutions in the course of asserting their Americanism, could sympathize with all rebellions against British authority, and were inclined to support the doctrine of Manifest Destiny. In spite of this, the Irish Americans along with the Southern slave holders formed part of the coalition which made up the Democratic party, but it was among the abolitionists, prohibitionists, and nativists outside the party that interest in the annexation of Canada was to be found.

As the Patriotes in Lower Canada and the Reformers in Upper Canada were tinged with nativism, the Irish immigrants to Canada in the 1830s became part of the loyalist coalition, which included Orangemen and Tories, and took a leading part in putting down the rebellions of 1837. They thus acquired a stake in the loyalist tradition which the Canadian Fenians were reluctant to renounce in the 1860s.

This prevalence of nativism among North American radicals not only explains Irish Canadian loyalism in 1837, but is the probable explanation for the absence of an effective liaison between Irish nationalists in the United States and the Hunters Lodges. There is a parallel between W. L. Mackenzie, who used nativist propaganda before 1837, courting the Irish Americans in 1839, and the former Know-Nothing candidate, Nathaniel Banks, seeking the Irish vote in 1866.

The Hunters in their declining years made efforts to find a base among the Irish Americans and, with the revival of Irish republicanism in 1848, Irish American nationalists threatened to invade Canada. Although these threats never went beyond speeches at public meetings and received no encouragement from Canadian annexationists, the threats caused Lord Elgin some anxiety. Had it not been for the sudden and complete collapse of the insurrection in Ireland in 1848, Irish republicans in the United States might have anticipated the Fenians by using the resources of the military clubs they controlled to launch raids against Canada.

Yet the Irish republicanism of 1848, which had drawn its impulse from the republican revival in Europe, could not survive the collapse of European revolutions. Even the republican exiles in America did not attempt to launch a new conspiracy until the outbreak of the Crimean War aroused hopes of receiving Russian assistance. In seeking the support of Imperial Russia, the Irish acted independently of Catholic opinion and international republicanism. The allied war effort was not only supported by the Pope but also received the moral support of international revolutionaries such as Karl Marx who hoped to see the end of Czarist influence in Europe.

At the end of the Crimean War, the Irish republican organization in America again dissolved, and it was evident that no organization could be created in America without a parallel movement in Ireland. It was with this in mind that James

Stephens was selected to draw together the republican sympathies which were presumed to exist in Ireland and was
promised American financial support.

Stephens had been a minor figure in the rising of 1848 who
had spent some time among continental revolutionaries. He
took pride in his understanding of revolutionary technique
but was prepared, if necessary, to sacrifice his republicanism
if, in so doing, he would secure support from Napoleonic
France. Although capable of denouncing clerical influence in
politics, Stephens never showed the antipathy towards the
church displayed by Mitchel and O'Mahony.

A man of energy, intelligence, and, within limits, good
judgment, Stephens was perhaps the best possible choice for
the task of creating a revolutionary movement in Ireland. He
had a gift for winning the confidence of peasants and artisans,
but was less successful with the intellectuals of '48, and his
distaste for American society was something of a handicap. His
greatest asset as Fenian leader was that he would not recognize the impossibility of his task.

From the beginning, Stephens received from the American
organization barely enough to cover his personal expenses,
but the prestige of trans-Atlantic associations and the hope of
substantial aid were great compensations. Without further
assistance, he gathered sufficient followers during the first
years of the movement to organize and control the MacManus
funeral demonstration. This appears to have been the high
point of his influence and demonstrated the limits of the kind
of activity he could carry out. His inability to make effective
use of the money and trained officers sent to Ireland in 1865
suggests that even had O'Mahony sent all the assistance
Stephens requested, the authorities would have been able to
seize most of the funds and arrest most of the officers.

What Stephens was attempting was to create an institutionalized revolutionary movement which would secure a monop-
oly on agitation by the disruption of constitutional meetings
in Ireland. Demonstrations would be regarded as a rehearsal
for the ultimate rising, but would differ little from those
organized by O'Connell. This creation of an illegal organization to carry on legal demonstrations could only be justified

if there were some hope of a rising in the near future. To sustain this hope, Stephens had to encourage expectation of imminent action which was invariably deferred. The size and voluntary character of his organization made security impossible and the authorities could disrupt his preparations for a rising whenever they appeared to constitute a threat to law and order.

Had British authority undergone the kind of suspended animation that afflicted continental governments in 1848, Stephens's preparations might have matured to the point where a rising was possible. Yet it does not appear that he considered such a crisis a prerequisite for success. He was ready to attack whenever he considered his forces to be properly armed and commanded.

It was not part of Fenian calculations to win concessions by mere threats of insurrection, but they claimed that concessions made were the result of their threats and this claim may have had some basis in fact. Constitutionalists attempted to strengthen the case for reform by pointing to the revolutionary alternative. Yet these threats, often used when no formal revolutionary organization existed, were less formidable than the Irish bloc vote in the British parliament which no British cabinet could ignore. Moreover, the failure of the projected uprising in 1865 and the fizzle in 1867 deprived such threats of their force.

The American Fenian organization was, in theory, a voluntary organization dedicated to raising money and training men for a rising in Ireland. In practice, although the organization did provide moral support and publicity for the Irish movement, the social activities and the secretariat of the organization consumed much of the money raised. Until the outbreak of the American Civil War, the kind of training acquired in the various Fenian military organizations in the United States was of little use to Stephens because the need for trained men could be met more easily by means of former soldiers of the British army.

With the Civil War this changed and, after the initial disruption of the organization caused by Fenian enlistments, O'Mahony became titular head first of a vast body of serving soldiers, and then of trained veterans. It was now possible to send experienced officers and considerable sums of money to Ireland, but not without the knowledge of the authorities. Although Archibald and McMicken, who conducted most of the Anglo-Canadian secret service work, were able men, it was informers who provided the most useful information. Only Le Caron, who volunteered to infiltrate the movement, was in any sense a British agent.

At nearly every point, the secrets of the inner councils of Fenians were known to the authorities, the notable exception being the raid of June 1866 when the Fenians were to some extent protected by the breakdown of their plans and the spontaneous action of O'Neill. Stephens's refusal to countenance reprisals against informers was wise in a movement where charges of treason were made without evidence and in which the unpopular were more likely to suffer than the guilty. As most of the informers came into the movement through the American organization, it is reasonable to assume that Stephens was a fair judge of character and may have profited by his experience among continental secret societies. O'Mahony was easily deceived, as were other leaders of the American movement who were soldiers and politicians with no experience of clandestine work. There does not appear to have been any organized counter-intelligence work within the Fenian system and adventurers were placed in positions of trust as soon as they had won the confidence of American leaders.

As Fenianism was essentially a climate of opinion, sustained by propaganda, the help of informers was indispensable in making the distinction between mere propaganda and serious preparations for action. As this climate of opinion extended to Canada, where there were no useful informers among the small group of committed Fenians, McMicken's agents soon discovered that Fenian sympathizers had neither the intention nor the means of becoming a threat.

D'Arcy McGee and Moylan understood this instinctively, but they feared with good reason that Fenian propaganda was damaging to the prestige and perhaps the safety of the Irish Canadian community. John A. Macdonald seems to have taken the same view. Both Brown and the Orangemen realized that Canadian Fenians did not constitute a serious threat, but they were infuriated by Boyle's editorials and consequently were not averse to arousing Fenian Fever as a means of curtailing his audacity. McGee and Moylan looked upon Boyle as irresponsible and said so when they thought it was necessary, but for the most part they did not wish to attract attention to the Fenian presence among Irish Canadians.

McGee's version of a "new Canadian nationality" called for the ultimate assimilation of the Irish and immediate renunciation of aggressive measures in disputes with the Orangemen. This was not of much use to McGee who had to make his way in politics by means of the Irish bloc vote. Moreover, the idea that "American Republicanism" was demoralizing the Irish population in the United States was not popular among Irish Canadians who found Bishop Lynch's denunciation of British policy in Ireland more congenial.

Lynch's insistence that Irish nationality was being destroyed in Ireland and consequently had to be asserted by the Irish overseas suited the needs of the Fenians. So, too, did the Hibernian Society, where military exercises carried out for defence against Orangemen were regarded by the initiated as preparations for an Irish uprising. Although taken seriously by those who participated in them, the military exercises were, in practice, one of the many social activities of the Hibernians, like the annual excursion to Niagara. They helped to create a sense of participating in events in Ireland and the United States which Toronto Fenians could read about in the *Irish Canadian*.

Although not a Fenian himself, Boyle attempted in the *Irish Canadian* to evolve a policy by which Fenians in Canada could remain loyalist while supporting rebellion in Ireland. At first he supported the Irish Constitutionalists, unaware, perhaps, that Stephens was attacking them in Ireland. By degrees, Boyle came to advocate physical force in Ireland although still stressing Irish attachment to the monarchy and accusing Brown of republican sympathies. Even after the Chicago Fenian convention, Boyle endeavoured to deny the republican character of Fenianism and was able to retain the confidence of Bishop Lynch throughout 1864.

The nocturnal demonstration of November 4 in Toronto was a blunder which not only aroused Fenian Fever among Protestants, but raised doubts in Bishop Lynch's mind about the judgment of Boyle and Murphy. Efforts to regain Lynch's confidence by remaining indoors on March 17, 1865 were nullified by James MacDermott's republican oratory, while Murphy's attack on Bishop Farrell of Hamilton provided the occasion for an open break between the Toronto Hibernians and Bishop Lynch in the autumn of 1865. The break with the bishop which deprived the Toronto Hibernians of their last link with respectability came just when news reached Canada of the raid on the office of the *Irish People* in Dublin and rumours began to circulate about Fenian raids on Canada. Consequently, this relative isolation of the Hibernians seemed less important to them than the rising power of the American Fenian movement and the belief in an imminent rising in Ireland.

This belief in the existence of an Irish rising also sustained O'Mahony throughout the schism in the movement until the spring of 1866. The support he received from Canadian Fenians owed less to his rejection of the invasion project than to the fact that he was the father of American Fenianism while his rival, Roberts, was little known in Canada. O'Mahony would have done better to have left the initiative for an attack on Canada to Roberts. Yet the Campo Bello scheme might have had some propaganda value if the Fenians had inflicted or suffered casualties. Its total failure was the result of MacDermott's information to British authorities which destroyed all hope of a surprise attack.

Campo Bello was ideally designed to turn the tide in favour of Confederation, but it also induced Canadian authorities to underestimate the potential of the armed veterans of the Roberts wing of Fenianism. These men, led by experienced officers, were formidable. Even had they not been favoured by the fortunes of war at Ridgeway, the fact of having crossed the frontier and engaged British forces could have been exploited by the Fenian press just as the trials of prisoners taken during the raid provided more opportunities for propaganda than the victory itself.

From the raids of 1866 it was clear that the American politicians would temporize with the Fenians, but in the end the neutrality laws would be enforced. It was also clear that the Fenian presence imposed humiliation and anxiety on American military and civil authorities in the border areas. They would therefore act against the Fenians at the earliest possible moment, even if it meant anticipating orders from Washington.

Although the battle of Ridgeway seemed to justify further action along the frontier, American opinion would not permit an immediate resumption of the raids. Yet Congress treated the Fenian vote with respect and there would be no American interference with the preparations for insurrection in Ireland.

It seems likely that had Stephens retained control of the movement there would have been no Fenian rising in 1867 or, perhaps, at any time. The talents of the Irish American officers had to be employed quickly if they were to be used at all. Like Stephens, they made plans for a general rising, but were prepared to act without much preparation and would continue to act if their plans went wrong. Although the leadership was supplied by Irish Americans, the real base now of the movement's activities was in the Midlands of England. As there was still no substantial financial support from America, they hoped to seize arms from the stores of the military and police. The inability of Kelly to co-ordinate the actions of his followers was perhaps an advantage, because his plans were known to the authorities.

The clashes with the police in March 1867 had been inspired by a plan which broke down. Yet they served to assert the existence of armed resistance to British authority in Ireland. Nothing more could be done, and for such assertions no general plan was necessary. Episodes like the rescue of Kelly and the Clerkenwell explosion served just as well to keep the movement alive as perpetual plans for a general uprising.

The organization of the Clan-na-Gael suggests that this was understood by some Fenians in 1867. Yet there was no concerted effort to adopt the methods of the twentieth-century Irish Republican Army, possibly because of negative reaction to the Clerkenwell explosion among the Fenians themselves.

The rising of 1867 marked the climax of Irish Fenianism. The organization which Stephens had created had finally gone beyond legal demonstrations and mere preparations for illegal action. In the course of doing so, it destroyed itself. Yet Stephens's methods could not be kept up indefinitely and the rising, along with Ridgeway, secured for the Fenians a place in Irish folklore which could not have been achieved by mere preparations and demonstrations.

During the Canadian election of 1867, McGee referred to the "carcase of Fenianism". In a sense, he was right, but defeated movements can be dangerous, especially when they are virtually leaderless and can find shelter within a respectable political party. McGee had to face the fury of miscellaneous Montreal Fenians who needed someone to blame for defeat. Whelan was typical of minor Fenian personalities who made the movement a force on street corners and in taverns, and it is not surprising that he or a group of his friends decided to go beyond talk to avenge defeat.

By this time, Toronto Fenianism was already in decline and McGee's funeral, which was in effect an anti-Fenian demonstration of the Montreal Irish community, excluded the possibility of making Whelan's defence a means of rallying Fenian support. Sir John A. Macdonald recognized that there were still Fenian sympathizers in Canada but, as there was no longer a movement to sympathize with, he saw in them nothing more than potential voters for the conservative coalition.

The raid of 1870 was the final gesture of the Fenian military clubs which by this time had evolved into veterans' associations. O'Neill could rally several hundred half-hearted Fenians who still respected him as the victor of Ridgeway. The Fenians and the groups which grew out of them like the Clan-na-Gael would survive, as would the idea of raids against Canada which was revived in 1914. Among their plans was a scheme for the building of a Fenian submarine designed to attack British commerce when war was expected between Britain and Russia in 1878.

In Canada, small groups of Irish republicans lingered on, providing a conspiratorial way of life for a limited number of Irish Canadians. Irish republican volunteers rode with Boer commandos in South Africa and efforts were made on one occasion to induce Spain to attack Gibraltar. Yet after 1870, Constitutionalism again dominated Irish politics and attracted the sympathy and interest of the main body of Irish nationalists in North America.

The Irish presence in the United States meant that in time there would be projects for the Americanization of Irish politics. There was really no way that this could be done because American politics did not produce parliamentary agitators like O'Connell and Parnell whom the Irish might emulate. It was equally difficult to re-enact the American Revolution in Ireland because this demanded conspiracy which in turn led to clandestine politics far removed from the American tradition.

Irish emigrant politicians who hoped to rise in American politics would have to adopt an American style which many could not or would not acquire. McGee solved the problem by going to Canada where the O'Connellite style of politics was acceptable. O'Mahony and his associates created a trans-Atlantic fraternal organization which sought to institutionalize the idea of Irish revolution. The threat posed by this organization imposed vast expenditure for security in Ireland and British America, and was a source of anxiety to American politicians dependent upon the Irish vote. In the area of Anglo-American relations, the presence of Fenianism created serious tension. In the British province, although it provided a much-needed tonic to loyalism on the eve of Confederation, it caused both acute embarrassment to loyalists among the Irish Canadians and the divisions within the Irish Canadian community that led to the assassination of D'Arcy McGee.

At the end of the American Civil War, the Fenians had acquired vast resources—wealth, American votes, and military talent—which enabled them to create tension on both sides of the Atlantic. For five years these resources remained under the control of various Fenian factions, all sustained by the myth of their ability to strike a blow against the British Empire, either in Ireland or in Canada. With the failure of the Fenian rising in Ireland in 1867 and the collapse of O'Neill's raid into Canada in 1870, the myth was dispelled and the movement it had sustained disintegrated.

# Notes

PAC: Public Archives of Canada
PAO: Public Archives of Ontario

CHAPTER ONE

1. Thomas D'Arcy McGee, *A History of the Irish Settlements in North America from the earliest period to the Census of 1850* (Boston, 1855), pp. 23-26.
2. Ibid., pp. 23, 27.
3. R. A. Billington, *The Protestant Crusade* (Gloucester, Mass., 1963), pp. 8, 13.
4. Hereward Senior, *Orangeism in Ireland and Britain 1795-1836* (London, 1966), pp. 2-4.
5. Billington, *The Protestant Crusade*, p. 16.
6. Ibid., p. 13.
7. Senior, *Orangeism in Ireland and Britain*, p. 5.
8. Maurice R. O'Connell, *Irish Politics and Social Conflict in the Age of the American Revolution* (Philadelphia, 1965), pp. 25-26.
9. Mason Wade, *The French Canadians* (Toronto, 1955), p. 65.
10. Billington, *The Protestant Crusade*, p. 19.
11. John Francis Maguire, *The Irish in America* (London, 1868),

pp. 353-54; Billington, *The Protestant Crusade*, pp. 20-23.

12. McGee, *Irish Settlements*, p. 51.

13. S. D. Morrison, *The Oxford History of the American People* (New York, 1965), p. 236.

14. S. Watson, *The Reign of George III* (London, 1963), pp. 133-34.

15. Donald Riel, "Chartism in Manchester", in *Chartist Studies*, ed. Asa Briggs (London, 1959), pp. 50-52.

16. P. Guilday, *Life and Times of John England* (New York, 1927), p. 7; Maguire, *Irish in America*, p. 357.

17. Senior, *Orangeism in Ireland and Britain*, pp. 26-27.

18. Ibid., p. 139.

19. P. J. Foik, "Anti-Catholic Parties in American Politics, 1776-1860", in *Records of the American Catholic Historical Society of Philadelphia* (Philadelphia, March 1925), p. 45; Billington, *The Protestant Crusade*, pp. 23-24.

20. Sir Thomas Liston to Sir Robert Prescott, May 23, 1799, cited in McGee, *Irish Settlements*, p. 88.

21. *Dictionary of American Biography* (New York, 1931), VI, pp. 145-46.

22. Ibid., VII, pp. 153-54.

23. McGee, *Irish Settlements*, pp. 94-95.

24. Gerald Craig, *Upper Canada, the Formative Years 1784-1841* (Toronto, 1963), p. 98; Edith Firth, *Town of York* (Toronto, 1966), p. lxxii.

25. *Shamrock, or Hibernian Chronicle* (New York, May 30, 1812).

26. Ibid. (July 4, 1812).

27. Ibid. (September 19, 1812).

28. Maguire, *Irish in America*, pp. 444-46; Billington, *The Protestant Crusade*, p. 24.

29. Maguire, *Irish in America*, p. 376; Billington, *The Protestant Crusade*, p. 37.

30. Billington, *The Protestant Crusade*, p. 37.

31. Guilday, *Life and Times of John England*, p. 920; *Dictionary of American Biography*, VI, pp. 161-63.

32. John England, *The Works of the Right Reverend John England, First Bishop of Charleston* (Cleveland, 1908), VI, pp. 388-486.

33. Billington, *The Protestant Crusade,* pp. 47-48.

34. James D. Horan and H. Swiggett, *The Pinkerton Story* (New York, 1951), p. 135.

35. E. R. Norman, *History of Modern Ireland* (Miami, 1971), pp. 67-74.

36. PAC, Mondelet Papers, MG24/1327, Minute Book 1827-34, p. 280; see also letter to editor, signed "Old Friend of Ireland", in the *Vindicator* (Montreal, March 14, 1837).

37. L. Whitney, *The Burning of the Convent* (Boston, 1877); Billington, *The Protestant Crusade,* pp. 68-76.

38. Maguire, *Irish in America,* pp. 413-14; Billington, *The Protestant Crusade,* pp. 99-108; for Montreal reaction, see *Transcript* (Montreal, March 4, 1837 and April 4, 1837).

39. Wade, *The French Canadians,* p. 143.

40. Ibid., p. 145.

41. Jacques Monet, "E. B. O'Callaghan", in *Dictionary of Canadian Biography* (Toronto, 1972), X, p. 554.

42. Aileen Dunham, *Political Unrest in Upper Canada, 1815-1836* (Toronto, 1963), pp. 123-24.

43. Hereward Senior, "Ogle Gowan and the Immigrant Question", in *Ontario History* (Toronto, December 1974), pp. 197-98.

44. Elinor Senior, "An Imperial Garrison in its Colonial Setting: British Regulars in Montreal 1832-54", unpublished Ph.D. thesis, McGill University (1976), pp. 20-34; Helen Taft Manning, *The Revolt of French Canada* (Toronto, 1962), pp. 344-54.

45. Senior, "Ogle Gowan and the Immigrant Question", pp. 204-05.

46. Monet, "E. B. O'Callaghan", pp. 554-55.

47. Carman Miller, "John Ponsonby Sexton", in *Dictionary of Canadian Biography,* X, pp. 646-47.

48. Head to Glenelg, September 22, 1837, in Charles R. Sanderson, *The Arthur Papers* (Toronto, 1957), I, p. 31.

49. Mackenzie's *British, Irish and Canadian Gazette* (Rochester, N.Y., April 6, 1839).

50. Oscar A. Kinchen, *The Rise and Fall of the Patriot Hunters* (New York, 1956), pp. 11-27.

51. Ibid., pp. 20-22, 37-38.

52. Ibid., pp. 63, 70.

53. Ibid., pp. 55-59.

54. E. A. Theller, *Canada in 1837-38* (Philadelphia, 1841), I, pp. 212-14.

55. Ibid., II, pp. 246-65; *Statesman* (Kingston, December 1, 1838); clipping from the *Albion* (New York, November 17, 1838), in PAC, Papineau Papers, MG24/B157/122; E. B. O'Callaghan to *Falconer*, November 22, 1838, in PAC, Chapman Papers, MG24/B31, I, p. 64.

56. *Mackenzie's Gazette* (October 26, 1839).

57. Ibid. (March 14, 1840 and March 28, 1840).

58. Kinchen, *The Rise and Fall of the Patriot Hunters,* p. 33.

59. Ibid., p. 120.

60. T. A. Pulby to M. S. Bartlett, October 10, 1841, in ibid., p. 112.

61. McGee, *Irish Settlements,* p. 133.

62. Ibid., pp. 144-47; Maguire, *Irish in America,* p. 439; Billington, *The Protestant Crusade,* p. 224.

63. Maguire, *Irish in America,* p. 441.

64. Billington, *The Protestant Crusade,* pp. 232-39.

65. Ibid., pp. 238-39.

66. Morrison, *Oxford History of the American People,* p. 564.

CHAPTER TWO

1. Thomas D'Arcy McGee, *A History of the Irish Settlements in North America from the earliest period to the Census of 1850* (Boston, 1855), p. 176; R. A. Billington, *The Protestant Crusade* (Gloucester, Mass., 1963), pp. 325-36.

2. McGee, *Irish Settlements,* p. 180.

3. John Francis Maguire, *The Irish in America* (London, 1868), pp. 438-58; Billington, *The Protestant Crusade,* pp. 380-97.

4. Isabel Skelton, *The Life of Thomas D'Arcy McGee* (Gardenvale, N.Y., 1925), pp. 10-29.

5. John O'Leary, *Recollections of Fenians and Fenianism* (London, 1896; reprinted, Shannon, 1969), I, pp. 29-38.

6. McGee, *Irish Settlements,* p. 134; William D'Arcy, *The Fenian Movement in the United States 1858-1886* (New York, 1947), p. 5.

7. Sir Arthur Doughty, ed., *The Elgin-Grey Papers 1846-52* (Ottawa, 1937), I, p. 150.

8. Ibid., pp. 160, 166.

9. Ibid., p. 205.

10. Elgin to ——, July 18, 1848, in T. Walrond, ed., *Letters and Journals of the Earl of Elgin* (London, 1872), pp. 57-58; see also *Pilot* (Montreal, July 18, 1848).

11. Elgin to Grey, August 16, 1848, in Doughty, *Elgin-Grey Papers,* I, pp. 223-25.

12. New York *Herald* article, reprinted in *Pilot* (Montreal, July 29, 1848); PAO, Mackenzie-Lindsey Papers, clipping no. 3001 taken from Mackenzie's *Volunteer* (July 29, 1848).

13. Major Robert Sanders to Assistant Adjutant General, Montreal, August 1, 1848, in PAC, RG8/C860/32.

14. Elgin to Grey, August 16, 1848, in Doughty, *Elgin-Grey Papers,* I, p. 225.

15. Ibid.

16. Ibid.

17. Ibid.

18. Elgin to Grey, November 16, 1848, in Doughty, *Elgin-Grey Papers,* I, p. 257.

19. J. H. Whyte, *Independent Irish Party 1850-1859* (Oxford, 1958), pp. 24-26.

20. Josephine Phelan, *The Ardent Exile* (Toronto, 1951), pp. 94-95.

21. Skelton, *McGee,* pp. 22-23.

22. Ibid., pp. 177-78.

23. Ibid., p. 178.

24. McGee, *Irish Settlements,* p. 191.

25. Maguire, *Irish in America,* pp. 554, 573; John Devoy, *Recollections of an Irish Rebel* (New York, 1929; reprinted, Shannon, 1969), pp. 266-68; O'Leary, *Recollections,* I, p. 100.

26. Skelton, *McGee,* p. 196.

27. Ibid.

28. Ibid., p. 199.

29. D'Arcy, *Fenian Movement,* p. 4.

30. Ibid., p. 5.

31. Ibid., p. 7.

32. Joseph Denieffe, *Personal Narrative of the Irish Revolutionary Brotherhood* (New York, 1906), p. 3.

33. D'Arcy, *Fenian Movement,* p. 8.

34. Skelton, *McGee,* pp. 271-74.

35. Ibid., p. 207.

36. Ibid., p. 210.

37. Ibid., p. 211.

38. Ibid., p. 268.

39. Ibid., p. 207.

40. Desmond Ryan, *The Fenian Chief: A Biography of James Stephens* (Dublin, 1967), pp. 1-34.

41. Ibid., p. 362; O'Leary, *Recollections,* I, pp. 100-04.

42. Ryan, *The Fenian Chief,* p. 236.

43. Ibid., pp. 57-66.

44. Ibid., pp. 96-101.

45. O'Leary, *Recollections,* I, pp. 111-12.

46. Michael Davitt, *Fall of Feudalism in Ireland* (New York, 1904; reprinted, Shannon, 1970), p. 77.

47. O'Leary, *Recollections,* I, pp. 119-33.

48. Ibid., I, pp. 120-21; Ryan, *The Fenian Chief,* p. 91; Mabel Walker, *The Fenian Movement* (Colorado Springs, 1969), p. 7.

49. O'Leary, *Recollections,* I, p. 84, see footnote.

50. Stephens to Doheny, January 1, 1858, in Denieffe, *Irish Revolutionary Brotherhood,* pp. 159-60.

51. O'Leary, *Recollections,* I, p. 89.

52. Ibid., pp. 94-95.

53. D'Arcy McGee to Gavan Duffy, May 8, 1849, in Gavan Duffy, *My Life in Two Hemispheres* (London, 1898; reprinted, Shannon, 1968), II, pp. 5-6.

54. Ryan, *The Fenian Chief,* p. 126.

55. Ibid., p. 105.

56. Ibid., pp. 131-40.

57. Ibid., p. 149.

58. T. D. McGee, "An Account of the Attempts to Establish Fenianism in Montreal", in the *Gazette* (Montreal, August 17, 1867).

59. Donal McCartney, "The Church and the Fenians", in Maurice Harmon, ed., *Fenians and Fenianism* (Dublin, 1968), pp. 13-20.

60. D'Arcy, *Fenian Movement,* p. 16.

61. Ibid., pp. 16, 28.

62. Ryan, *The Fenian Chief*, pp. 232-33.
63. D'Arcy, *Fenian Movement*, pp. 18-20.
64. Ryan, *The Fenian Chief*, pp. 75-76.
65. Denieffe, *Irish Revolutionary Brotherhood*, p. 71.

CHAPTER THREE

1. Robin Burns, "D'Arcy McGee and the Fenians", in Maurice Harmon, ed., *Fenians and Fenianism* (Dublin, 1968), pp. 74-75; Josephine Phelan, *The Ardent Exile* (Toronto, 1951), p. 47; Isabel Skelton, *The Life of Thomas D'Arcy McGee* (Gardenvale, N.Y., 1925), pp. 281-83.
2. Skelton, *McGee*, p. 327.
3. Ibid., p. 335.
4. Thomas D'Arcy McGee, *The Irish Position in British and Republican America* (Toronto, 1866), pp. 15-16.
5. Skelton, *McGee*, p. 337.
6. McGee to O'Donohoe, March 9, 1859, in PAC, MG1/A6, 14291.
7. Joseph Denieffe, *Personal Narrative of the Irish Revolutionary Brotherhood* (New York, 1906), p. 25.
8. *Canadian Freeman* (Toronto, August 17, 1865).
9. William D'Arcy, *The Fenian Movement in the United States 1858-1886* (New York, 1947), p. 202.
10. Ibid.
11. Skelton, *McGee*, p. 368.
12. PAC, Moylan Papers, MG29/D15; Phelan, *The Ardent Exile*, p. 164.
13. H. C. McKeown, *Life and Labors of Most Reverend John Joseph Lynch, First Archbishop of Toronto* (Toronto, 1886), pp. 279-81, 300-02.
14. E. R. Norman, *The Catholic Church in Ireland in the Age of the Rebellion 1859-1873* (London, 1965), p. 112; Donal McCartney, "The Church and the Fenians", p. 15; Peadar MacSuibhne, *Paul Cullen and his Contemporaries* (Naas, Ireland, 1961-1973), IV, p. 319.
15. *Irish Canadian* (Toronto: February 26, 1863; April 22, 1863; May 13, 1863; June 17, 1863; June 24, 1863).
16. McKeown, *Life of Lynch*, pp. 225-26.

17. McGee to Moylan, November 8, 1860, in PAC, Moylan Papers, MG29/D15; Phelan, *The Ardent Exile*, pp. 187-89.

18. Phelan, *The Ardent Exile*, p. 195.

19. *Gazette* (Montreal, December 23, 1861).

20. *Canadian Freeman* (Toronto, October 11, 1865); *Irish Canadian* (Toronto, January 28, 1863).

21. Thomas D'Arcy McGee, "An Account of the Attempts to Establish Fenianism in Montreal: A Memoir", in the *Gazette* (Montreal, August 17, 1867).

22. Ibid. (December 26, 1861).

23. Ibid. (August 17, 1867).

24. John O'Leary, *Recollections of Fenians and Fenianism* (London, 1896; reprinted, Shannon, 1969), I, p. 172; Denieffe, *Irish Revolutionary Brotherhood*, pp. 73-74.

25. Stephens to O'Mahony, April 7, 1862, cited in D'Arcy, *Fenian Movement*, p. 26.

26. D'Arcy, *Fenian Movement*, pp. 16-21.

27. Ibid., p. 28.

28. Denieffe, *Irish Revolutionary Brotherhood*, pp. 78-79; Mabel Walker, *The Fenian Movement* (Colorado Springs, 1969), p. 21.

29. *Globe* (Toronto, March 18, 1862).

30. *Canadian Freeman* (Toronto, March 20, 1862).

31. *Irish Canadian* (Toronto, January 7, 1863).

32. Ibid. (January 28, 1863); for McGee's attitude, see *Irish Canadian* (August 10, 1864).

33. Ibid. (March 25, 1863; April 1, 1863).

34. Ibid. (February 25, 1863).

35. D'Arcy, *Fenian Movement*, p. 29.

36. *Irish Canadian* (Toronto, March 18, 1863).

37. Ibid. (March 25, 1863).

38. *Globe* (Toronto, March 21, 1863).

39. *Irish Canadian* (Toronto, March 25, 1863).

40. Ibid. (April 1, 1863).

41. Ibid. (April 22, 1863).

42. Ibid. (May 27, 1863).

43. Ibid. (June 10, 1863); *Gazette* (Montreal, August 31, 1863).

44. Ibid. (June 17, 1863).

45. *Globe* (Toronto, July 16, 1863).

46. *Irish Canadian* (Toronto, July 22, 1863).

47. Ibid. (August 26, 1863).

48. MacSuibhne, *Cullen,* IV, p. 150.

49. Bishop Ignace Bourget, *Mandements, lettres, pastorales, circulaires et autres documents* (Montreal, 1887), V, p. 67, see "l'Encyclique Quanto conficiamur moerore (10 août 1863)"; see also IV, p. 386, "Lettre pastorale des Pères du Troisième Concile provinciale de Québec (21 mai 1863)".

50. *Gazette* (Montreal, August 17, 1867).

51. *Irish Canadian* (Toronto, September 2, 1863).

52. Ibid. (October 21, 1863).

53. Ibid. (November 4, 1863).

54. *Leader* (Toronto, November 25, 1863).

55. *Irish Canadian* (Toronto, November 11, 1863).

56. D'Arcy, *Fenian Movement,* p. 33; Walker, *The Fenian Movement,* p. 21.

57. D'Arcy, *Fenian Movement,* p. 36; Walker, *The Fenian Movement,* p. 22; D'Arcy's figures are based on the O'Mahony papers; Walker gives 326, based on newspaper reports.

58. *Globe* (Toronto, December 16, 1864).

59. D'Arcy, *Fenian Movement,* pp. 35-36.

60. Ibid., p. 38.

61. Desmond Ryan, *The Fenian Chief: A Biography of James Stephens* (Dublin, 1967), pp. 191-92; D'Arcy, *Fenian Movement,* p. 36.

62. D'Arcy, *Fenian Movement,* p. 34.

63. O'Mahony to C. J. Kickham, October 4, 1863, in ibid., p. 32; Cullen to Kirby, December 3, 1863, in MacSuibhne, *Cullen,* IV, p. 158.

64. D'Arcy, *Fenian Movement,* p. 37.

65. Walker, *The Fenian Movement,* p. 52; *Hansard,* Gt. Bt., CLXXXIII 891, Papers relating to foreign affairs, 1865-66, Pt. II, pp. 103-04.

66. D'Arcy, *Fenian Movement,* p. 38.

67. Ibid., pp. 39-40, 49; Walker, *The Fenian Movement,* pp. 25-26.

68. *Irish Canadian* (Toronto, November 18, 1863).

69. Ibid. (January 13, 1864).

70. *Canadian Freeman* (Toronto, February 11, 1864).

71. *Irish Canadian* (Toronto, August 17, 1864).

72. Donal McCartney, "The Church and the Fenians", p. 16.

73. *Irish Canadian* (January 27, 1864).

74. Ibid. (February 17, 1864).

75. Ibid. (March 23, 1864); *Globe* (Toronto, March 18, 1864).

76. *Irish Canadian* (Toronto, March 18, 1864).

77. *Canadian Freeman* (Toronto: March 21, 1864; April 7, 1864); *Patriot* (Toronto, March 19, 1864).

78. *Irish Canadian* (Toronto, January 20, 1864).

79. Ibid. (March 30, 1864).

80. *Canadian Freeman* (April 14, 1864); McGee to editor of *Leader* (Toronto), reprinted in *Patriot* (Toronto, April 13, 1864).

81. *Irish Canadian* (April 27, 1864).

82. Ibid. (May 25, 1864).

83. *Canadian Freeman* (Toronto: April 14, 1864; May 5, 1864; June 16, 1864).

84. *Irish Canadian* (Toronto, June 1, 1864).

85. Ibid.

86. Ibid. (June 8, 1864).

87. O'Leary, *Recollections,* II, p. 31.

88. *Irish Canadian* (Toronto, August 31, 1864); MacSuibhne, *Cullen,* IV, p. 172; Norman, *The Catholic Church in Ireland,* pp. 138-39.

89. *Irish Canadian* (September 7, 1864).

90. *Canadian Freeman* (Toronto, November 10, 1864); *Leader* (Toronto, November 9, 1864).

91. *Irish Canadian* (Toronto, July 20, 1864).

92. *Canadian Freeman* (Toronto, November 9, 1864); *Patriot* (Toronto, November 9, 1864).

93. *Globe* (Toronto: November 7, 1864; November 9, 1864); *Canadian Freeman* (Toronto, November 17, 1864).

94. *Leader* (Toronto, November 8, 1864).

95. Ibid. (November 9, 1864).

96. *Globe* (Toronto, November 8, 1864); *Irish Canadian* (Toronto, November 9, 1864).

97. *Globe* (Toronto, November 19, 1864).

98. *Irish Canadian* (November 16, 1864); *Leader* (November 9, 1864).

99. *Leader* (November 12, 1864).

100. *Globe* (November 12, 1864; November 16, 1864); *Leader* (November 16, 1864).

101. *Leader* (November 9, 1864; November 10, 1864; November 11, 1864).

102. *Irish Canadian* (November 16, 1864); *Leader* (November 15, 1864).

103. *Globe* (November 18, 1864).

104. *Irish Canadian* (November 23, 1864).

105. Ibid. (November 9, 1864).

106. Ibid. (November 23, 1864).

107. *Globe* (December 19, 1864; December 20, 1864); *Leader* (December 9, 1864; December 10, 1864; December 14, 1864).

108. *Irish Canadian* (December 14, 1864).

109. *Patriot* (December 14, 1864).

110. *Irish Canadian* (December 14, 1864).

111. *Globe* (December 19, 1864; December 20, 1864).

112. *Leader* (December 16, 1864).

113. Lord Monck to Sir Fenwick Williams, private, December 8, 1864, in New Brunswick Museum, Saint John, Fenwick Williams Papers, IV.

114. *Irish Canadian* (December 21, 1864); see also *Loyal Orange Association Annual Proceedings* (1865), pp. 10, 18.

115. *Irish Canadian* (February 1, 1865).

116. Ibid. (November 15, 1864).

117. *Irish Canadian* (November 23, 1864).

118. *Leader* (December 29, 1864).

119. *Irish Canadian* (January 18, 1865); *Gazette* (Montreal, January 12, 1865).

120. *Canadian Freeman* (March 21, 1864; April 7, 1864).

121. McGee to Moylan, private, October 22, 1865, in PAC, Moylan Papers, MG29/D15.

122. *Irish Canadian* (January 11, 1865; January 18, 1865).

123. Ibid. (February 8, 1865); *Canadian Freeman* (March 23, 1865).

124. D'Arcy, *Fenian Movement*, pp. 47-48.

125. *Irish Canadian* (August 17, 1864; November 2, 1864).

126. Ibid. (November 2, 1864).

127. Ryan, *The Fenian Chief*, pp. 202-03; E. M. Archibald to Lt. General Sir John Michel, December 20, 1865, in PAC, RG7/G10/I, Secret Despatches 1865-66.

128. *Globe* (March 18, 1865).

129. *Irish Canadian* (March 29, 1865).

130. *Dublin Evening Mail* (May 16, 1865) .

131. Ibid.


CHAPTER FOUR


1. John Devoy, *Recollections of an Irish Rebel* (New York, 1929; reprinted, Dublin, 1969), pp. 128-32; Leon O Broin, *Fenian Fever: An Anglo-American Dilemma* (New York, 1971), pp. 33-51; Desmond Ryan, *The Fenian Chief: A Biography of James Stephens* (Dublin, 1967), p. 214; A. J. Semple, "The Fenian Infiltration of the British Army", in *Journal of the Society for Army Historical Research* (London, Autumn 1974), LIII, no. 211, pp. 133-60.

2. Hereward Senior, *Orangeism in Ireland and Britain 1795-1836* (London, 1966), pp. 200, 227.

3. Devoy, *An Irish Rebel*, pp. 41-46; John O'Leary, *Recollections of Fenians and Fenianism* (London, 1896; reprinted, Shannon, 1969), I, pp. 250-66.

4. O Broin, *Fenian Fever*, pp. 15-16; Ryan, *The Fenian Chief*, pp. 206-07, 210-11.

5. Brian Jenkins, *Fenians and Anglo-American Relations during Reconstruction* (Ithaca, N.Y., 1969), p. 72; O Broin, *Fenian Fever*, pp. 20-21.

6. Devoy, *An Irish Rebel*, p. 41.

7. William D'Arcy, *The Fenian Movement in the United States 1859-1886* (New York, 1947), p. 60.

8. For money sent to Ireland, see *Irish American* (June 9, 1865), cited in D'Arcy, *Fenian Movement*, p. 73.

9. Devoy, *An Irish Rebel*, pp. 69-70.

10. *Irish Canadian* (Toronto: September 13, 1865; September 20, 1865).

11. E. M. Archibald to Earl Russell, October 31, 1865, in PAC, RG7/G10/I, 1865-66; O Broin, *Fenian Fever*, pp. 52-53; D'Arcy, *Fenian Movement*, pp. 83-84.

12. Jenkins, *Fenians and Anglo-American Relations*, pp. 134-45.

13. D'Arcy, *Fenian Movement*, pp. 36, 47.

14. E. M. Archibald to Sir John Michel, November 1, 1865, in PAC, RG7/G10/I, Secret Despatches 1865-66, encl. extract from a secret despatch to Earl Russell, October 31, 1865; *Fenian Progress: A Vision and the Constitution of the Fenian Brotherhood* (New York, 1865), pp. 71-90.

15. *Fenian Progress,* pp. 71-90.

16. D'Arcy, *Fenian Movement,* p. 107.

17. Mabel Walker, *The Fenian Movement* (Colorado Springs, 1969), p. 63.

18. *Irish People* (Dublin, June 9, 1866), cited in D'Arcy, *Fenian Movement,* p. 181.

19. Walker, *The Fenian Movement,* pp. 62-63.

20. For a summary of American press reaction, see D'Arcy, *Fenian Movement,* pp. 104-06.

21. Ibid., pp. 107-10.

22. Ibid., p. 111; W. S. Neidhardt, *Fenianism in North America* (University Park, 1975), pp. 33-34.

23. *Herald* (New York, March 27, 1866), cited in D'Arcy, *Fenian Movement,* p. 128.

24. O Broin, *Fenian Fever,* pp. 26-27; Devoy, *An Irish Rebel,* pp. 69-70, 77.

25. For a copy of this circular, see *Morning News* (Saint John, N.B., March 12, 1866).

26. *Herald* (New York, March 5, 1866), cited in D'Arcy, *Fenian Movement,* p. 124.

27. Ibid., pp. 105, 133.

28. Jenkins, *Fenians and Anglo-American Relations,* pp. 134-35.

29. Ibid.

30. *Irish Canadian* (March 22, 1865); *Canadian Freeman* (May 23, 1865); *Globe* (March 18, 1865).

31. *Irish Canadian* (June 8, 1864).

32. Ibid. (April 27, 1864).

33. *Canadian Freeman* (August 3, 1865).

34. Ibid.

35. Ibid. (August 10, 1865).

36. Ibid. (August 17, 1865).

37. *Irish Canadian* (August 9, 1865).

38. Ibid.

39. Ibid. (August 23, 1865).

40. *Globe* (August 17, 1865).
41. *Irish Canadian* (September 13, 1865; September 20, 1865; September 27, 1865).
42. *Canadian Freeman* (October 23, 1865).
43. *Irish Canadian* (November 1, 1865).
44. Neidhardt, *Fenianism in North America*, p. 31.
45. *Leader* (October 28, 1865).
46. See Gowan's letter in *Irish Canadian* (November 8, 1865).
47. *Irish Canadian* (November 22, 1865).
48. *Canadian Freeman* (November 9, 1865).
49. Resolution of the Grand Lodge of Lower Canada, in *Leader* (November 10, 1865).
50. *Canadian Freeman* (November 30, 1865; December 14, 1865; January 18, 1866); see also Robert McGee, "The Toronto Irish Catholic Press and Fenianism, 1863-66", unpublished MA thesis, University of Ottawa (1969), pp. 34-36.
51. *Irish Canadian* (February 14, 1866).
52. *Canadian Freeman* (January 4, 1866).
53. Ibid. (January 25, 1866).
54. Ibid. (February 1, 1866).
55. Ibid. (March 1, 1866).
56. *Irish Canadian* (February 7, 1866).
57. Ibid. (March 7, 1866).
58. *Globe* (March 9, 1866).
59. Michael Murphy to editor, *Globe* (March 12, 1866).
60. D'Arcy, *Fenian Movement*, p. 135.
61. *Globe* (March 12, 1866).
62. *Irish Canadian* (March 14, 1866).
63. McGee to Brown, private, *c.* March 1866, in PAC, RGI/A2/1429.
64. Monck to Macdonald, March 13, 1866, in PAC, Macdonald Papers, Vol. 74, 28846-49; T. P. Slattery, *They Got To Find Mee Guilty Yet* (Toronto, 1972), p. 301.
65. *Canadian Freeman* (March 15, 1866).
66. Ibid.
67. Michael Murphy to editor, *Globe* (March 12, 1866).
68. C. P. Stacey, "A Fenian Interlude: The Story of Michael Murphy", in *Canadian Historical Review* (June 1934), XV, p. 143.
69. For Gowan's account of the parade and Fenian intentions,

see Gowan to John A. Macdonald, March 19, 1866, in PAC, Macdonald Papers, MG26A/458/22806-67.

70. *Canadian Freeman* (March 17, 1866).

71. *Irish Canadian* (March 21, 1866).

72. Josephine Phelan, *The Ardent Exile* (Toronto, 1951), pp. 255-56.

73. *Irish Canadian* (March 21, 1866).

74. For Fenian preparations against Campo Bello, see *Morning News* (Saint John, N.B., April 11, 1866); see also PAC, RG8/C1672, Fenian telegrams, April 9, 1866 to April 11, 1866.

75. *Irish Canadian* (December 21, 1864).

76. *Canadian Freeman* (January 25, 1866).

77. W. S. MacNutt, *New Brunswick 1784-1867* (Toronto, 1963), p. 427.

78. *Morning Freeman* (Saint John, N.B.: April 21, 1866; May 3, 1866); *The Reporter* (Fredericton, N.B., April 27, 1866).

79. P. B. Waite, *The Life and Times of Confederation 1864-7: Politics, Newspapers and the Union of British North America* (Toronto, 1962), p. 227.

80. Ibid., pp. 261-62.

81. D'Arcy, *Fenian Movement*, p. 135.

82. Maj. General Sir Hastings Doyle to Sir Fenwick Williams, April 20, 1866, in PAC, RG8/C1262, 193.

83. Capt. A. H. Hood to Vice Admiral Sir James Hope, April 11, 1866, in PAC, RG8/C1272; Commander of the Forces to Hon. Arthur Gordon, April 11, 1866 and April 15, 1866, in ibid., Waite, *Life and Times of Confederation*, p. 267.

84. For diplomatic correspondence surrounding this incident, see Jenkins, *Fenians and Anglo-American Relations*, pp. 137-39; Neidhardt, *Fenianism in North America*, pp. 47-48; Sir Hastings Doyle to Sir Fenwick Williams, April 20, 1866, in PAC, RG8/C1672/193; Harold A. Davis, "The Fenian Raid on New Brunswick", in *Canadian Historical Review* (December, 1955), XXXVI, pp. 316-34.

85. Maj. General Sir Hastings Doyle to Lieutenant Governor Arthur Gordon, April 15, 1866, in PAC, RG8/C1272.

86. Sir Fenwick Williams to Sir Hastings Doyle, April 21, 1866, in PAC, RG8/C1672.

87. Hon. A. Gordon to Sir Hastings Doyle, April 16, 1866, in PAC, RG8/C1672.

88. Col. Cole to Doyle, April 14, 1866, in PAC, RG8/C1672; Robert Kerr, Eastport, to Col. Anderson, April 9, 1866, in ibid.

89. *Morning News* (Saint John, N.B., March 19, 1866); *Morning Freeman* (Saint John, N.B.: April 21, 1866; May 3, 1866).

90. *Morning News* (Saint John, N.B., April 23, 1866), reprinted from the Eastport *Sentinel; The Reporter* (Fredericton, N.B., April 27, 1866).

91. *Morning Freeman* (Saint John, N.B., April 21, 1866); Waite, *The Life and Times of Confederation*, p. 213.

92. *Le Pays* (Montreal, May 22, 1866).

93. D'Arcy, *Fenian Movement*, p. 151.

94. *Canadian Freeman* (May 10, 1866).

95. Canada: *Sessional Papers*, no. 75 (1869), p. 64.

96. H. W. Hemans to Lord Lyon, November 12, 1865, cited in D'Arcy, *Fenian Movement*, p. 65.

97. J. E. Wilkins to F. D. Adams, August 19, 1865, in ibid., p. 86.

98. Edith Archibald, *Life and Letters of Sir Edward Mortimer Archibald* (Toronto, 1929), pp. 166-74.

99. O Broin, *Fenian Fever,* pp. 47-50.

100. J. A. Macdonald to J. Cockburn, January 2, 1865, in PAC, MG26A/510, letter-book VII, pp. 165-66.

101. J. A. Macdonald to Gilbert McMicken, September 22, 1865, in ibid., 511, letter-book VIII, pp. 259-60; McMicken to Macdonald, April 30, 1866, in ibid., MG26A/237/103628-33.

102. Sir John Michel to Macdonald, October 13, 1865, in PAC, MG26A/56/22301-04.

103. Sir John Michel to Cardwell, October 23, 1865, in PAC, RG7/G21/i.

104. Scott to Macdonald, December 4, 1865, in PAC, MG26A/56/22503-07.

105. Archibald to Michel, November 1, 1865, in PAC, RG7/G3/ii.

106. Monck to Macdonald, November 10, 1865, in PAC, MG26A/74/28818-20.

107. Jenkins, *Fenians and Anglo-American Relations*, p. 107.

108. Archibald to Michel, December 20, 1865, in PAC, RG7/G3/ii.

109. P. C. Burton (Nolan) to McMicken, December 31, 1865, in PAC, MG26A/237/103131-34.

110. McLeod to John Simpson, February 28, 1866, encl. McLeod to Macdonald, March 12, 1866, March 19, 1866, March 21,

1866, in PAC, MG26A/57/22692/700, 22725-28, 22795-98, 22799-803.

111.  McMicken to Macdonald, May 17, 1866, in PAC, MG26A/237/103745-48.

112.  D'Arcy, *Fenian Movement*, p. 163.

113.  McMicken to Macdonald, May 17, 1866, in PAC, MG26A/237/103745-48.

114.  Hemans to McMicken, May 19, 1866, May 26, 1866, in PAC, MG26A/237/103761-64, 103799-803.

115.  Macdonald to Duncan McKay, May 19, 1866, in ibid., 512, letter-book IX, p. 234.

116.  General T. W. Sweeny's address to the Pittsburgh Fenian convention, in Joseph Denieffe, *Personal Narrative of the Irish Revolutionary Brotherhood* (New York, 1906), p. 270.

117.  Richard Slattery to General Sweeny, May 9, 1866, in ibid., pp. 236-37.

118.  Official report of General T. W. Sweeny, Secretary of War, Fenian Brotherhood, and Commander in Chief of the Irish Republican Army, September 1866, cited in Denieffe, *Irish Revolutionary Brotherhood*, pp. 255-62.

119.  D'Arcy, *Fenian Movement*, p. 146.

120.  Official report of General Sweeny, September 1866, cited in Denieffe, *Irish Revolutionary Brotherhood*, p. 258.

121.  Facsimile of General Sweeny's Proclamation, cited in John A. Macdonald, *Troublous Times in Canada, a History of the Fenian Raids of 1866 and 1870* (Toronto, 1910), p. 30; also printed in *Le Pays* (Montreal, June 9, 1866).

122.  J. Mackay Hitsman, *Safeguarding Canada 1763-1871* (Toronto, 1968), p. 201.

123.  Neidhardt, *Fenianism in North America*, p. 64.

124.  There is considerable material on the battle of Ridgeway. Neidhardt, *Fenianism in North America*, pp. 59-65, gives the most comprehensive account based on recent research. For Lt.-Col. Booker's first account of the battle, see his letter to Major General G. Napier, June 2, 1866, in *The Canada Gazette* (Ottawa, June 23, 1866).

125.  Macdonald, *Troublous Times in Canada*, p. 92.

126.  D'Arcy, *Fenian Movement*, pp. 164-67.

127.  *Le Pays* (Montreal: June 9, 1866; June 12, 1866); Neidhardt, *Fenianism in North America*, pp. 76-84.

CHAPTER FIVE

1. *Irish Canadian* (Toronto, July 6, 1866).
2. Brian Jenkins, *Fenians and Anglo-American Relations during Reconstruction* (Ithaca, N.Y., 1969), pp. 198-99.
3. William D'Arcy, *The Fenian Movement in the United States 1859-1886* (New York, 1947), pp. 217-18.
4. Jenkins, *Fenians and Anglo-American Relations*, p. 228.
5. *The New York Times* (June 4, 1866), cited in Jenkins, *Fenians and Anglo-American Relations,* p. 94; *Irish Canadian* (June 20, 1866).
6. *Leader* (Toronto, June 5, 1866); *Globe* (Toronto, June 7, 1866).
7. *La Minerve* (Montreal, January 17, 1867).
8. *Le Pays* (Montreal, June 9, 1866).
9. *Irish Canadian* (June 6, 1866; June 13, 1866).
10. *Canadian Freeman* (Toronto: June 14, 1866; June 21, 1866).
11. Ibid. (October 8, 1866).
12. W. S. Neidhardt, *Fenianism in North America* (University Park, 1975), p. 108.
13. *Irish Canadian* (November 9, 1864; November 22, 1865).
14. *Canadian Freeman* (March 8, 1866).
15. Ibid. (November 11, 1866).
16. Ibid. (November 15, 1866).
17. *Irish Canadian* (November 2, 1866).
18. *Canadian Freeman* (November 29, 1866).
19. *Cincinnati Enquirer* (December 15, 1866), cited in Mabel Walker, *The Fenian Movement* (Colorado Springs, 1969), p. 173.
20. *Irish Canadian* (April 18, 1866); C. P. Stacey, "A Fenian Interlude: The Story of Michael Murphy", in *Canadian Historical Review* (June, 1934), pp. 147-51.
21. *Globe* (December 5, 1866; December 7, 1866; December 11, 1866; December 14, 1866; December 19, 1866; December 29, 1866); *Canadian Freeman* (December 14, 1866; December 21, 1866).
22. D'Arcy, *Fenian Movement*, p. 182.
23. Walker, *The Fenian Movement,* p. 108.
24. D'Arcy, *Fenian Movement*, pp. 186-88.
25. *Irish Canadian* (August 24, 1866).

26. D'Arcy, *Fenian Movement*, p. 189.

27. *Tablet* (New York, September 15, 1866); ibid., p. 190.

28. Walker, *The Fenian Movement*, p. 112.

29. D'Arcy, *Fenian Movement*, p. 199.

30. Neidhardt, *Fenianism in North America*, p. 101.

31. John Mitchel to O'Mahony, March 10, 1866, cited in Joseph Denieffe, *Personal Narrative of the Irish Revolutionary Brotherhood* (New York, 1906), p. 221.

32. Leon O Broin, *Fenian Fever, An Anglo-American Dilemma* (New York, 1971), p. 111.

33. Desmond Ryan, *The Fenian Chief: A Biography of James Stephens* (Dublin, 1963), pp. 238-39.

34. John Rutherford, *The Secret History of the Fenian Conspiracy* (London, 1877), II, pp. 259-60.

35. Ibid., p. 257.

36. Ryan, *The Fenian Chief*, pp. 243-46.

37. *Dictionary of American Biography* (New York, 1934), XVI, p. 20.

38. O Broin, *Fenian Fever*, pp. 121-23.

39. Ibid., pp. 126-29.

40. Ibid., p. 127; John Devoy, *Recollections of an Irish Rebel* (New York, 1929; reprinted, Dublin, 1969), p. 269; Denieffe, *Irish Revolutionary Brotherhood*, p. 141.

41. D'Arcy, *Fenian Movement*, p. 221.

42. Thomas N. Brown, *Irish-American Nationalism 1870-1890* (Philadelphia and New York, 1966), p. 22; Ryan, *The Fenian Chief*, p. 243.

43. Devoy, *An Irish Rebel*, pp. 187-89; O Broin, *Fenian Fever*, pp. 127-29.

44. Devoy, *An Irish Rebel*, p. 189.

45. Kevin Nowlan, "The Fenian Rising of 1867", in T. W. Moody, ed., *The Fenian Movement* (Cork, 1968), pp. 23-35; Devoy, *An Irish Rebel*, pp. 190-234; Denieffe, *Irish Revolutionary Brotherhood*, pp. 138-43.

46. O Broin, *Fenian Fever*, pp. 174-75.

47. Devoy, *An Irish Rebel*, pp. 237-39; Jenkins, *Fenians and Anglo-American Relations*, pp. 320-21.

48. Devoy, *An Irish Rebel*, pp. 244-47; O Broin, *Fenian Fever*, pp. 194-200.

49. O Broin, *Fenian Fever*, pp. 203-29.

50. Ibid., pp. 210-11; for a description of Ricard Burke, see Devoy, *An Irish Rebel*, pp. 347-49.

51. O Broin, *Fenian Fever*, p. 214.

52. Devoy, *An Irish Rebel*, pp. 210-11; O Broin, *Fenian Fever*, p. 217.

53. Rutherford, *Fenian Conspiracy*, II, pp. 309-10; O Broin, *Fenian Fever*, pp. 222-26.

54. O Broin, *Fenian Fever*, p. 220.

55. D'Arcy, *Fenian Movement*, p. 231.

56. Denieffe, *Irish Revolutionary Brotherhood*, pp. 129-30; Devoy, *An Irish Rebel*, pp. 190-91.

57. D'Arcy, *Fenian Movement*, pp. 233-34.

58. *Dictionary of American Biography*, I, p. 578.

59. D'Arcy, *Fenian Movement*, pp. 234-36.

60. Ibid., p. 249; Walker, *The Fenian Movement*, p. 144.

61. Devoy, *An Irish Rebel*, pp. 235-36; Walker, *The Fenian Movement*, p. 146.

62. Neidhardt, *Fenianism in North America*, p. 111; D'Arcy, *Fenian Movement*, p. 164.

63. Peter Toner, "The Military Organization of the Canadian Fenians 1866-1870", in *The Irish Sword* (Dublin, Summer 1971), X, no. 38, p. 34; Ryan, *The Fenian Chief*, p. 236; D'Arcy, *Fenian Movement*, pp. 260-61.

64. Henri Le Caron, *Twenty Years in the Secret Service* (Boston, 1892), p. 28.

65. J. M. S. Careless, *Brown of the Globe* (Toronto, 1963), II, p. 246; Luther Holton to Brown, June 21, 1867, in PAC, Brown Papers, MG24/B40; Luther Holton to Brown, July 28, 1867, in PAC, MG1/A2/1614-17.

66. T. P. Slattery, *The Assassination of D'Arcy McGee* (Toronto, 1968), pp. 401, 405.

67. *Canadian Freeman* (March 21, 1867).

68. *Irish Canadian* (January 15, 1868).

69. *Canadian Freeman* (June 6, 1867; June 27, 1867; July 4, 1867; July 11, 1867; July 18, 1867).

70. Hereward Senior, "Quebec and the Fenians", in *Canadian Historical Review* (March 1967) XLVIII, no. 1, p. 31.

71. Ibid., p. 37.

72. Elinor Senior, "An Imperial Garrison in its Colonial Setting: British Regulars in Montreal 1832-54", unpublished Ph.D. thesis, McGill University (1976), pp. 21-24.

73. Ibid., pp. 295, 299, 305, 310, 315-18, 321, 396-441.

74. Robin Burns, "D'Arcy McGee and the New Nationality", unpublished MA thesis, Carleton University (1966), p. 78.

75. Slattery, *The Assassination*, p. 403.

76. Ibid., pp. 409-10.

77. Senior, "Quebec and the Fenians", pp. 37-39.

78. Ibid., p. 38.

79. Gazette (August 17, 1867; August 20, 1867; August 22, 1867).

80. Slattery, *The Assassination*, p. 414.

81. *True Witness* (Montreal, September 13, 1867); *La Minerve* (September 7, 1867).

82. Loyola University, Excerpts from Diary of George E. Clerk, dated October 2, 1867.

83. *Gazette* (August 17, 1867).

84. Slattery, *The Assassination*, p. 428.

85. Ibid., pp. 429-30.

86. Ibid., pp. 434-36.

87. Burns, "D'Arcy McGee and the New Nationality", p. 58; Slattery, *The Assassination*, p. 442.

88. Senior, "Quebec and the Fenians", p. 40; T. P. Slattery, "Patrick James Whelan", in *Dictionary of Canadian Biography*, IX, p. 835.

89. *La Minerve* (September 16, 1868), for Whelan's statement at the close of the trial; T. P. Slattery, *They Got to Find Mee Guilty Yet* (Toronto and Garden City, N.Y., 1972), p. 55.

90. Senior, "Quebec and the Fenians", pp. 40-41.

91. Testimony of Joseph Faulkner, Montreal tailor, and Alex Turner at Whelan's trial, in *True Witness* (September 10, 1868); see also testimony of James Inglis, in *La Minerve* (September 10, 1868).

92. Testimony of McGee's brother at trial, *True Witness* (September 10, 1868); testimony of Alex Turner, *La Minerve* (September 10, 1868); see also Whelan's statement at the close of his trial, in *La Minerve* (September 16, 1868).

93. *Irish Canadian* (February 11, 1869).

94. Slattery, *They Got to Find Mee Guilty Yet*, pp. 329-38.

95. *Irish Canadian* (February 11, 1869); see also opinion of editor, *Herald* (Montreal, September 16, 1868).

96. Gilbert McMicken to Sir John A. Macdonald, March 9, 1870, in PAC, MG26A/244; A. McMicken to G. McMicken, March 29, 1870, ibid.; O Broin, *Fenian Fever*, p. 238.

97. Michael Davitt, *Fall of Feudalism in Ireland* (New York, 1904; reprinted, Shannon, 1970), pp. 255-63.

98. *Irish Canadian* (April 8, 1868).

99. Senior, "Quebec and the Fenians", p. 42.

100. *Irish Canadian* (September 2, 1868).

101. Ibid. (September 9, 1868).

102. Ibid. (March 17, 1869; March 24, 1869).

103. Rutherford, *Fenian Conspiracy*, II, p. 301; Denieffe, *Irish Revolutionary Brotherhood*, pp. 276-77; John Devoy, *Devoy's Post Bag 1871-1928*, eds. William O'Brien and Desmond Ryan (Dublin, 1948-53), I, p. 3.

104. C. J. Coursol, Commissioner, Dominion Police, to Sir John A. Macdonald, April 1, 1870, confidential, in PAC, MG26A/244; Le Caron, *Twenty Years in the Secret Service*, pp. 60-70; D'Arcy, *Fenian Movement*, pp. 334-36.

105. R. G. Sagen (alias Le Caron, Thomas Beach) to James Bell, January 21, 1870, in PAC, MG26A/244.

106. Ibid.

107. G. McMicken to Sir John A. Macdonald, February 12, 1870, in PAC, MG26A/244.

108. C. J. Coursol to Sir John A. Macdonald, April 1, 1870, confidential, in PAC, MG26A/244.

109. McMicken to Sir John A. Macdonald, March 9, 1870 in PAC, MG26A/244; *Gazette* (Montreal, March 2, 1870).

110. *Evening Star* (Montreal, May 25, 1870); *Le Pays* (Montreal, 27 mai 1870); Neidhardt, *Fenianism in North America*, pp. 116-17.

111. Macdonald, *Troublous Times in Canada*, pp. 159-61.

112. Neidhardt, *Fenianism in North America*, pp. 121-23.

113. Devoy, *Devoy's Post Bag*, I, pp. 4-24.

114. A. G. Morice, *History of the Catholic Church in Western Canada* (Toronto, 1910), II, pp. 72-73.

115. Sir John A. Macdonald to Frank Smith, July 17, 1871, confidential, in PAC, MG26A/571, letter-book 16/40.

# Bibliographical Note

Material on Fenianism is infinite, but the most useful of the original sources dealing with its Canadian aspects are found in the Sir John A. Macdonald Papers at the Public Archives of Canada and in the files of the Toronto *Irish Canadian* and *Canadian Freeman*. There is extensive memoir material dealing with Fenianism, the most relevant being John Devoy's *Recollections of an Irish Rebel*, John O'Leary's *Recollections of Fenians and Fenianism*, and Henri Le Caron's *Twenty Years in the Secret Service*.

Colonel C. P. Stacey has written a number of articles touching on Fenianism and Canadian public opinion and security. Of these, the most important are "Fenianism and the Rise of National Feeling in Canada at the Time of Confederation" in the *Canadian Historical Review* (September 1931), and "A Fenian Interlude: the Story of Michael Murphy", which appeared in the June 1934 issue of the same journal. Material on French-Canadian reaction to Fenianism can be found in my article, "Quebec and the Fenians" in the *Canadian Historical Review* (March 1967).

One of the best introductions to Fenianism is still John Rutherford's *Secret History of the Fenian Conspiracy*, a pioneer work hostile to Fenianism, which contains many errors, but not enough to justify the abuse of the author found in Fenian memoirs. Desmond Ryan's *The Fenian Chief* gives a good account of James Stephens, and William D'Arcy's *The Fenian Movement in the United States 1858-1886* provides a scholarly, detailed analysis of the American movement, based on original sources which include O'Mahony's private papers. Mabel Walker's *The Fenian Movement,* written earlier than D'Arcy's book but published later, is based on extensive newspaper research and provides a less comprehensive but more concise account.

The diplomatic aspects of Fenianism have been dealt with in detail in a recent monograph by Brian Jenkins in *Fenians and Anglo-American Relations during Reconstruction.* Leon O Broin's *Fenian Fever: An Anglo-American Dilemma,* making use of the Fenian Papers at Dublin Castle, has covered Irish Fenians and Fenian surveillance in the United Kingdom. In a thoroughly researched monograph, W. S. Neidhardt has provided, in *Fenianism in North America,* the most concise and recent account of the military aspects of the Fenian invasions of Canada. Additional information is provided in Peter Toner's article, "Military Organization of the 'Canadian' Fenians 1866-1870", while Robert F. McGee's *Fenian Raids on the Huntingdon Frontier, 1866-70* gives a detailed account of Fenian raids in this area.

Useful background material on the Irish Catholic press is found in Robert McGee's MA dissertation "The Toronto Irish Catholic Press and Fenianism 1863-1866" (unpublished thesis, University of Ottawa, 1969) . Isabel Skelton's *Life and Times of D'Arcy McGee* and Josephine Phelan's *The Ardent Exile* provide a good introduction to the life of McGee, but the best account is Robin Burns's "Thomas D'Arcy McGee: A Biography" (unpublished PH D thesis, McGill University, 1976) .

A discussion of the fragments of Fenianism which survived in Canada after 1870 can be found in Peter Toner and D. C. Lyne's "Fenianism in Canada, 1874-84", published in *Studia Hibernica* (Dublin, 1972).

# Index